On-Scene Guide for
CRISIS NEGOTIATORS

On-Scene Guide for
CRISIS NEGOTIATORS

Frederick J. Lanceley

CRC Press
Boca Raton London New York Washington, D.C.

Library of Congress Cataloging-in-Publication Data

Lanceley, Frederick J.
    On-scene guide for crisis negotiators / by Frederick J. Lanceley
       p. cm.
    Includes bibliographical references and index.
    ISBN 0-8493-0784-8 (alk. paper)
      1. Hostage negotiations. 2. Negotiation. 3. Suicide—Prevention.
    4. Crisis intervention (Psychiatry) I. Title.
HV6595.L36 1999
302.3—dc21
                                                       98-7492
                                                         CIP

This book contains information obtained from authentic and highly regarded sources. Reprinted material is quoted with permission, and sources are indicated. A wide variety of references are listed. Reasonable efforts have been made to publish reliable data and information, but the author and the publisher cannot assume responsibility for the validity of all materials or for the consequences of their use.

Neither this book nor any part may be reproduced or transmitted in any form or by any means, electronic or mechanical, including photocopying, microfilming, and recording, or by any information storage or retrieval system, without prior permission in writing from the publisher.

The consent of CRC Press LLC does not extend to copying for general distribution, for promotion, for creating new works, or for resale. Specific permission must be obtained in writing from CRC Press LLC for such copying.

Direct all inquiries to CRC Press LLC, 2000 N.W. Corporate Blvd., Boca Raton, Florida 33431.

Trademark Notice: Product or corporate names may be trademarks or registered trademarks, and are used only for identification and explanation, without intent to infringe.

© 1999 by CRC Press LLC

No claim to original U.S. Government works
International Standard Book Number 0-8493-0784-8
Library of Congress Card Number 99-28068
Printed in the United States of America   2 3 4 5 6 7 8 9 0
Printed on acid-free paper

Preface

Nothing in this book should be considered legal advice. Should the reader misconstrue anything in this book as being such, please be warned that the author is consistently wrong when he does attempt a legal opinion. The negotiator's best source of legal advice is his or her local prosecutor. (Actually, inviting a prosecutor to negotiation training sessions is an excellent idea.)

Neither should this book be considered a substitute for attending a seminar on crisis negotiation. The more seminars attended, the better. The more legitimate approaches a negotiator has to a particular problem, the greater the likelihood of success.

Negotiation is still an art. This book does not present the only way to accomplish any particular negotiation objective. Any one idea presented in this book may result in favorable outcomes 86 percent of the time, for example. The reader's current way of tackling the same problem might accomplish a favorable result 82 percent or even 88 percent of the time. There could be several good ways to achieve a specific objective. We, as negotiators, do not claim to know the one and only—or even the best—way of accomplishing any one end result.

Masculine pronouns will be used to describe subjects in this book for ease of reading and because the vast majority of people encountered in negotiated situations are male. Most negotiators estimate that the percentage of female subjects is fewer than 10 percent.

The illustrative stories or anecdotes in this book are all true. The author experienced them or they were related to him by one of the many of thousands of negotiators that he has had the privilege to work with over the years. An effort has been made to disguise the origin of the stories to preclude embarrassment to any negotiator or agency.

The Author

Frederick J. Lanceley retired from the Federal Bureau of Investigation after 26 years of government service including four years as an officer in the United States Air Force. During his many years assigned to the FBI Academy, he was the senior negotiator and principal director of their internationally acclaimed crisis-negotiation course. He has been involved in several hundred hostage, barricade, suicide, aircraft hijacking, and kidnapping cases. He has trained officers from every major law enforcement agency in the United States and more than 50 foreign countries, and has also presented hundreds of seminars and presentations around the world. He also conducted an important research project with the University of Louisville involving the study of aircraft hijacking.

Lanceley holds two master's degrees—an MBA from Texas Tech University and an M.S. in the administration of justice from California Lutheran College. He has also attended a wide variety of training sessions concentrating on topics related to crisis negotiation.

Fred Lanceley is a member of the American Foundation for Suicide Prevention, and the American Society of Law Enforcement Trainers. He was awarded an honorary life membership in the California Association of Hostage Negotiators for his contributions to the field of hostage negotiation. Because of his insights and innovative instructional methods, he has been described as one of the world's foremost authorities on the topic of crisis negotiation.

Lanceley has been qualified as an expert witness in federal and state courts on the topics of hostage/kidnap negotiation and victim experience and behavior. He has also consulted in a number of lawsuits that did not require actual testimony. He has appeared on several nationally televised programs both in the United States and abroad. He was an adjunct faculty member at the University of Virginia and is currently an adjunct professor at Daytona Beach

Table of Contents

Chapter I: The Problem in Perspective 1
   Crisis Negotiators Now Respond to a Variety of Situations 1
   Kidnapping 3
   Definitions 3
   Kidnapping — Unknown Location 4
   Kidnapping — Known Location 5
   Summary 6

Chapter II: Profiling Sieges 7
   Details on Siege Types and Characteristics 7

Chapter III: Crisis Intervention 13
   The Crisis State 13
   Crisis Characteristics 14
   Crisis Intervention 15
   The Purposes of Crisis Intervention 16

Chapter IV: Active Listening 17
   Active Listening Assumptions 17
   Active Listening Concepts 18
   Active Listening Skills 20
      Emotion Labeling 20
      Paraphrasing 21
      Reflecting or Mirroring 22
      Silence 22
      Minimal Encouragers 22
      "I" Messages 23
      Open-Ended Questions 23

Chapter V: Suicide Intervention 25
   Hostage Negotiators and Suicide Intervention 25
   Suicide Clues 26
   Determining Suicidal Intent 27
   Potential High Risk Indicators 28

Strange Stories and the Role of Fate..32
Suicide as a Problem-Solving Option...33
Communicating Suicidal Intent..33
Basic Concepts for Crisis Negotiators..34
Why Commit Suicide?...35
Determine Motivation...36
Ambivalence..36
Anger..36
Suicide-by-Cop..37
Indicators of Progress in Suicide Situations.................................39
When to Call a "Time Out" in Suicide Situations.......................39
Exposed Face-to-Face in Suicide Situations.................................39
Crisis Intervention Techniques..40
Negotiator Qualities..42

Chapter VI: Hostage Negotiation 43
Priorities..43
Courses of Action...43
Containment..44
Perimeters..44
What is Negotiable and What is Not...45
Suggested Negotiator Introduction..48
Common Means of Communication...51
The Role of Time..53
Stalling Techniques..53
Concerns that Arise with the Passage of Time............................54
Deadlines...57
Demands..57
Subject's Needs...59
Communication Recommendations..62
Double Check All Intelligence...63
Non-Response Situations..63
Hostage Injuries...65
The Stockholm Syndrome...65
Negotiators' Relationship to the Hostages and Victims............67
Medical Problems in High-Stress Situations...............................68
Common Subject Weaknesses..68
Telephone Negotiation Techniques...70
Tape Recording the Negotiation..70
Exposed Face-to-Face Considerations..71
Manipulation of Anxiety...73
Potential Problem Words and Phrases..73
Indicators of Negotiation Progress..74
Potential Problem Areas with the Media.....................................75

Use of Third Party Intermediaries 77
The "Boss" as Negotiator 81
Crisis Negotiation Team 82
Supplies/Equipment for Ready Kit 85
The Tactical Role of the Negotiator 86
Situation Boards 87
Negotiating the Non-Negotiable Situation 88
The Surrender 88
Before Deviating from Guidelines 90
The Effects of Negotiating on Negotiators 91
    Possible Short-Term Stressors and Problems 91
    Possible Long-Term Stressors and Problems 93

Chapter VII: Abnormal Psychology for Crisis Negotiators 95
Introduction 95
Antisocial Personality Disorder 97
    Characteristics 97
    Common Behaviors 98
    Communication Suggestions 98
Borderline Personality Disorder 99
    Characteristics 100
    Course 101
    Familial Pattern 101
    Common Behaviors 101
    Communication Suggestions 102
Schizophrenia 103
    Definitions 104
    Associated Features 106
    Age of Onset 106
    Impairment 106
    Complications 106
    Personality Prior to the Illness 107
    Predisposing Factors 107
    Prevalence 108
    Sex Ratio 108
    Course 108
    Familial Pattern 108
    Treatment/Medication 109
    Common Behaviors 109
    Communication Suggestions 110
Major Depressive Episode 111
    Associated Features 111
    Culture and Gender Features 111

Course 112
Common Behaviors 112
Treatment 114
Communication Suggestions 114

Appendix A: Suicide Intervention Flow Chart 119

Appendix B: Interview Guide for Investigators 125

Appendix C: Overview Active Listening Techniques .. 133

Appendix D: The Continuing Need for Training 137

Appendix E: The Dangers of Manipulating Anxiety Levels 141

Appendix F: The Negotiation Effort 147

Appendix G: The Troubled State of Crisis Management . 153

Appendix H: A Negotiator's View of the Incident at Ruby Ridge 159

Index 205

Chapter 1

The Problem in Perspective

Crisis Negotiators Now Respond to a Variety of Situations

In the early 1970s, in response to the threat of terrorism, the New York City Police Department (NYCPD) and a short time later, the Federal Bureau of Investigation (FBI), developed a hostage negotiation program. Captain Francis A. Bolz, Jr. and Harvey Schlossberg, Ph.D. (both now retired from NYCPD), and FBI instructors began teaching hostage negotiation courses to law enforcement agencies across the country. The concept caught on and very rapidly spread throughout the United States and into many other developed nations as well. By the late 1970s, it was becoming increasingly clear that, while many agencies now had hostage negotiation teams, few law enforcement agencies were actually encountering true hostage situations.

Hostage negotiation is composed of crisis intervention and bargaining techniques. As an equation, hostage negotiation equals crisis intervention plus bargaining. Most police departments were doing little, if any, bargaining, and, if any was done, it was over relatively minor issues such as cigarettes, telephone calls, etc. If bargaining is taken out of the equation, hostage negotiators become crisis interveners. If a negotiation team is not bargaining during a "typical" incident, their typical incident is almost certainly not a hostage situation.

A lieutenant of a major city was asked to describe a representative year for his negotiation team. He said, "Usually, we work two or three hostage situations—if we define the word "hostage" broadly. Then we work about six suicide incidents and about 50 barricades."

When asked what percentage of his barricades involved talk of suicide, he said that almost all of them had.

Explaining why he described the situations as "barricades" as opposed to "suicides," he said, "My guys would rather say they worked a 'man with a gun' call rather than a suicide. In fact, they were called out to a 'man with a gun,' but he just sat there all night crying to my negotiators about how his girlfriend had just left him and how he was considering suicide."

To the credit of law enforcement in the U.S. in the 1970s, the authorities started using the new hostage negotiation techniques. At that time, it was virtually their only nontactical option. Often, hostage negotiation techniques are not a perfect match for the variety of incidents faced by law enforcement negotiators.

Law enforcement negotiators encountered many suicidal individuals. To make matters worse, the suicidal persons they met were often at the most serious end of the spectrum concerning intent, i.e., they were very serious about actually going through with the suicide act. In these situations, police are forced to interact with desperate people who are sitting in their cars with guns in their mouths, or would-be jumpers who have climbed to the the top of a tall bridge, for example. While some suicide threats are merely gestures to gain attention to personal pain, the incidents police work often involve more than this. These individuals have been through that stage and their initial desperate attempts did not get them what they needed. Now they are much more intent and closer to going through with the suicide act.

Hostage negotiators worked many domestic situations. They were also dealing with spontaneous hostage situations, such as those in convenience stores, for example, that occasionally involved what later became known as suicide-by-cop. There were also a number of situations in high schools where a teenage gunman walked into a classroom, captured some of his classmates and typically demanded pizzas, cokes, and cigarettes.

The Problem in Perspective   **3**

Far less frequently, negotiators worked true hostage situations such as an embassy takeover by terrorists making demands on governments. FBI negotiators, in particular, also worked traditional kidnappings for ransom.

Kidnapping

The Federal kidnapping statute, Title 18, United States Code, Section 1201, reads, "Whoever unlawfully seizes, confines, inveigles, decoys, kidnaps, abducts, or carries away or holds for ransom or reward or otherwise any person ... shall be punished by imprisonment for any term of years or for life." This statute is similar to many state statutes. Kidnapping statutes are very broad in that if a person is being held against his or her will, that crime is generally prosecutable as a kidnapping regardless of the subject's intent. The term "kidnapping" then will be used here in a very broad sense and not just in the sense of a kidnapping for ransom.

In this volume, kidnappings are divided into two types. The first is one where the authorities do not know where the subject is located (see Figure 1.1.) The second is where the authorities know the location of the subject and have him contained. (See Figure 1.2.)

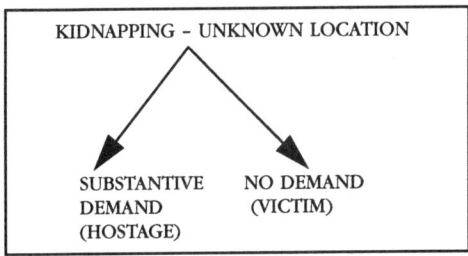

Figure 1.1

Definitions

Technically, a **hostage** is someone who is held and threatened by another person to force the fulfillment of substantive demands on a third party. In the media and even within law enforcement, the word

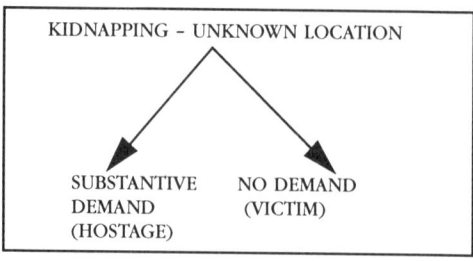

Figure 1.2

"hostage" is used very loosely. The word often means that someone is being held against his will and is surrounded by the police. For example, if law enforcement is working a domestic situation, the media often reports the incident as a "hostage" situation. While the wife or girlfriend in that domestic situation does not meet the definition of a true hostage, there is no other word in the English language that accurately describes her situation. What word is there to describe a person who is about to be murdered but has not been murdered as yet? There is none. She is a victim, but not a hostage.

A **substantive demand** is a demand that the subject has decided he cannot achieve by any other means. So, a hostage is a particular kind of kidnap victim, one for whom a substantive demand is made to facilitate his or her release. The hostage's value then is dependent on what the authorities, a corporation, or family is willing or able to pay in trade for his or her freedom.

A demand by the subject to make a telephone call to his mother or orders for cigarettes, beer, pizzas are not substantive demands. An individual does not have to take hostages to obtain pizza, beer, cigarettes, or talk to his mother. If there is no substantive demand, by definition, there is no hostage situation.

Kidnapping - Unknown Location

In this situation, the subject captures an innocent individual and takes him or her to an unknown location. If the subject makes a substantive demand upon a family, government, or corporation, we have a hostage situation. Generally, the substantive demand is for money, goods, political, or social change. No one kidnaps an innocent bystander off the street, takes him to an unknown location, and demands pizzas, cokes, and cigarettes. Negotiators would consider that situation ludicrous but yet, while working contained kidnapping situations, they often receive such demands and think nothing of it.

If there is no substantive demand, what might the subject's intent be? This kidnapping might be for the purposes of homicide, homicide/suicide, sexual assault, custodial or domestic disputes, religious or cult considerations, drug trade involvement, to intimidate, or other reasons. The innocent person here, though kidnapped, is a victim, not a hostage. A kidnapping often has no follow-up demand, as in the case of many women and children who are kidnapped off the street and assaulted. They are kidnap victims but not hostages.

Kidnapping — Known Location

In this instance, the subject is holding someone against his will but the authorities know where he is and have him contained (see Figure 1.2). The subject is making substantive demands that often involve demands that are very similar to kidnappings at unknown locations. However, in addition to demands for money, political and social change, there is now an escape demand. This is because the subject wants to get his demands met and get out of there. If there is no escape demand, the possibility of suicide and other dangerous outcomes should be considered.

If the subject and his victim are located but he makes no substantive demands, what might his intent be now? There are several possibilities. He might want to commit an assault, a sexual assault, a homicide, a homicide-suicide, a suicide-by-cop or he might simply intend to terrorize his victim.

In Figure 1.3 on page 9, Figures 1.1 and 1.2 are combined. On the left side of Figure 1.3 are hostage situations in locations that are both known and unknown to the authorities. In hostage situations, negotiators bargain with the subject because he wants something from the authorities, a family or corporation. In hostage situations, the family, victim or corporation is not powerless though it is often difficult for negotiators to convince them of that fact. The victimized corporation or family have something the subject wants and because they have something the subject wants, it gives them not only power but more control.

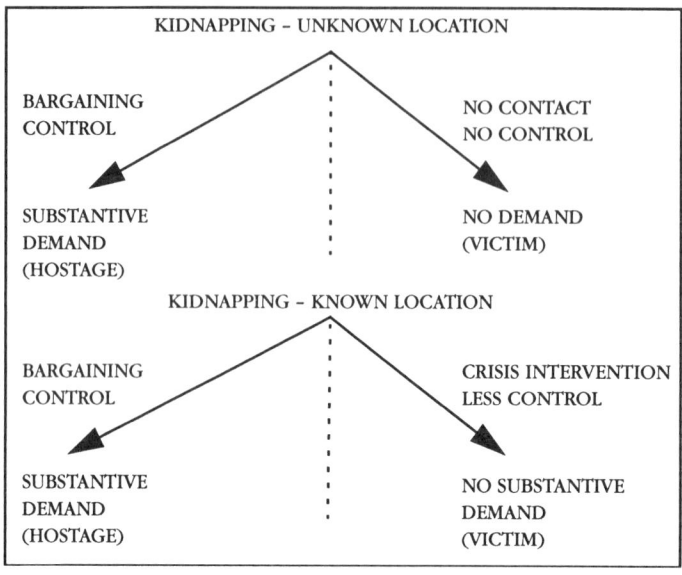

Figure 1.3 (Upper right), the authorities have no contact or control over the situation other than attempts to locate the subject and victim. This is a perilous situation in which the subject can perpetrate his crime with impunity, at least for the immediate future. (Lower right) the authorities cannot bargain because the subject wants nothing of substance from them. They have less control because they have only crisis intervention techniques at their disposal. In these incidents, the subject is often emotionally out of control and drugs and/or alcohol are exacerbating the situation.

Summary

Hostage situations allow some opportunity to the authorities, family, or corporation for control because they have something the subject wants, i.e., money or access to the power to get things done. True hostage situations are negotiated using crisis intervention and bargaining techniques. Non-hostage situations provide little or no opportunity to the authorities for control. They are negotiated using, primarily, crisis intervention techniques alone. The perpetrator wants nothing from the authorities; he has what he wants—the victim.

Chapter 2
Profiling Sieges

Sieges as described in this section are those incidents where a subject has barricaded himself in a location and there are innocent persons in the location with him. The degree of innocence varies widely. For example, the "innocent" person in some "domestic" incidents may actually be encouraging the subject in his actions, daring him to take action against the police just as he took action against her.

There are three basic types of sieges:

1. *Deliberate*: the perpetrator purposely sets out to initiate a siege situation. He is goading the authorities into responding because he wants something from them.
2. *Spontaneous*: the subject does something that inadvertently draws the attention of law enforcement. Often the authorities are responding to a call reported by an uninvolved party.
3. *Anticipated:* the subject expected that the government would come after him someday.

Details on Siege Types and Characteristics

As with any profile, the following is a generalization. Keep in mind that each person and situation has unique qualities. (See Table 2.1.)

Table 2.1 Siege Types and Characteristics

	Deliberate Sieges	Spontaneous Sieges	Anticipated Sieges
Substantive Demands	Yes	Not Often	No
Innocents	Hostages	Victims/Hostages	Followers, Family
Approach	Hostage Negotiation	Crisis Intervention	Active Listening
Duration	Long	Short	Long
Occurrence	Not Often	Common	Rare
Motivation	Political	Personal	Religious/Political
State of Mind	Rational	Emotional	Rational
Stance	Offensive	Defensive/Offensive	Defensive
Location	Public/Symbolic	Varies	Subject's Home
Number Of Subjects	Multiple	One	Multiple
Purposeful Timing	Yes	No	N/A
Preparation	Prepared	Unprepared	Prepared
Weapons	Complex, Portable	Readily Available	Complex
Ammunition	Sufficient	Minimal	Abundant
Drugs/Alcohol	No	Yes	No

Substantive Demands

A substantive demand is a one the subject feels he cannot achieve by any other means. Substantive demands are the *raison d'être* of hostage takers, i.e., the fulfillment of demands is the very reason for the siege. Spontaneous situations can involve substantive demands but usually do not. In spontaneous sieges, the authorities most commonly receive demands for more alcohol, drugs, to talk to friends, acquaintances or attorneys, cigarettes, pizza, etc. Anticipated sieges usually do not involve substantive demands.

Involvement of Innocents

Deliberate sieges do not involve family members. No one puts a gun to his wife's head and demands the overthrow of the government, the release of comrades from prison, a trip to Cuba, or any other substantive demand. Generally, there is no previous relationship between the subject and his victim.

On the other hand, in a spontaneous siege a drunken husband might put a gun to his wife's head and, when the authorities arrive, demand more beer. Spontaneous sieges most commonly involve persons known to the subject, including family members. However, on relatively infrequent occasions, spontaneous sieges will involve hostages. On these occasions, the subject is interrupted during the course of a crime and the hostage is taken to act as a shield or as a value to be traded for a means of escape. In anticipated sieges the innocents are family members, friends, or followers, who may be supportive or even urging the perpetrator on.

Approach

In deliberate sieges, law enforcement negotiators use a hostage negotiation approach because this involves crisis intervention and bargaining. In spontaneous sieges, negotiators use crisis intervention with a subject who is emotionally out of control. In anticipated sieges, the negotiator actively listens for topics of interest to the subject that the negotiator might use to resolve the incident. Wanting "nothing" from the authorities can actually make a situation more difficult. In anticipated sieges, there is often not much to talk about in that he wants nothing from the authorities except to get away and that is impossible.

Duration

Spontaneous sieges are relatively short in duration, generally only a few hours, since the subject is often in a crisis state. Deliberate and anticipated sieges are often much longer in duration, sometimes lasting several days. This is the result of several factors, including the subject's preparation, his expectations, and the relatively small emotional factor.

Occurrence

Spontaneous sieges are relatively commonplace, whereas deliberate sieges are rare and anticipated sieges rarer still.

Motivation

Historically, left-wing groups have taken hostages in deliberate sieges and right-wing groups or persons have been involved in anticipated sieges. The motivation for spontaneous sieges is usually emotional and personal.

State of Mind

In deliberate and anticipated sieges, the subject, while typically frightened, is relatively rational. Emotions, on the other hand, drive the spontaneous siege.

Stance

In deliberate sieges, the subjects take an offensive posture and, in anticipated sieges, they take a defensive posture. In spontaneous sieges, the subject's stance depends on how he responds to the situation. A few subjects respond aggressively and start making substantive demands, but more subjects respond with a variety of emotions and little else.

Location

The location for deliberate sieges is often a public or symbolic place. It might be, for example, the embassy or national airline of a hated nation. Spontaneous sieges can happen almost anywhere, but police respond to these incidents most commonly at the subject's residence. Anticipated sieges occur at the subject's residence because that is where the government could find him.

Number of Subjects

It is relatively uncommon for police departments or sheriff's offices to encounter more than one subject in a spontaneous siege. Multiple subjects in deliberate and anticipated sieges more often confront the FBI. In deliberate and anticipated sieges, there is often a strong leader but indictable followers.

Purposeful Timing

Deliberate sieges are sometimes initiated on special dates or anniversaries. Spontaneous sieges are just that, spontaneous. In anticipated sieges, the timing of the incident is at the government's judgment.

Preparation

In deliberate sieges, the subjects make what preparations they can before undertaking the siege. This preparation may be difficult in that they often have to travel to their target destination and carry their provisions with them. Subjects in anticipated sieges are the most prepared because they did anticipate this event. They are home and they are ready, in terms of food, water, weapons, ammunition, and mindset. Subjects in spontaneous sieges are unprepared for the event.

Weapons

Here, complex weapons are those that are at least semiautomatic. In deliberate sieges the subject(s) have to carry their weapons, often concealed, into a hostile environment. These circumstances limit what they can use during the siege. Subjects in spontaneous sieges use whatever is readily available as a weapon so the weaponry varies widely. Subjects often have complex and multiple weapons in anticipated sieges. They have had time to work on their preparation, so resources and creativity are their only limitations.

Ammunition

Subjects in deliberate sieges take with them whatever ammunition they feel will be sufficient. Subjects in anticipated sieges often have an abundance of ammunition. As the weaponry varies in spontaneous sieges, so does the ammunition.

Drugs/Alcohol

Drugs and/or alcohol are commonly seen in spontaneous sieges but are only seen in the other types of sieges if the subject(s) is taking them to stay awake.

Chapter 3

Crisis States and Crisis Intervention

The Crisis State

A crisis is any situation in which a person's ability to cope is exceeded. Often, the event that triggers a crisis state appears, to the negotiator, to be a minor occurrence. To the subject, however, that minor occurrence is often the final burden that he can no longer bear. The event becomes the proverbial straw that breaks the camel's back. Some examples are listed below to illustrate the point:

- A man shot and killed his neighbor because he believed the man was stealing steaks off his barbecue grill. He then committed suicide.
- A man arrived home to find his wife on the telephone telling her girlfriend about their family's financial difficulties. The husband overheard the conversation and said, "I wish you wouldn't tell everyone about our financial problems." He then went into their bedroom and shot himself.
- A young man in his mid-20s was suffering from severe back pain. He had recently undergone several operations and required two more. He was heavily medicated for the constant extreme pain. One afternoon, his mother arrived home to find

him drinking and admonished him. He then went into the bedroom and killed himself.
- An elderly male was afflicted with terminal cancer, going blind, and unable to control his bowels. His wife wanted to place him in a nursing home. One afternoon he accidentally broke a vase given to his wife by their daughter. When his wife berated him for breaking the vase, he put two guns to his head and threatened suicide. A negotiator persuaded him to surrender.
- A truck driver arrived home late one evening. Though his wife had already gone to bed, he asked if she would fix him something to eat. His wife said, "You did not do me the courtesy of telling me you were going to be late so I'm not fixing you anything." He turned off the light, climbed into bed, and lay down next to her. He then reached into the nightstand, pulled out a .357 magnum and fatally shot himself through the head.

Persons in a crisis state are being controlled by their emotions, not reason. Contrary to what is constantly heard in the media, people do not just "snap." There has been a build-up of psychological pain and stress that they could not relieve through their usual coping mechanisms.

In a way, stress build-up is a kind of mechanical process in that human beings are containers that "fill up" with stress. A person must be able to release stress occasionally or they will overflow with the input of additional stress and go into crisis. When coping mechanisms no longer reduce stress, people go into crisis.

Generally, there has been a precipitating event in the recent past. The subject perceives the situation to be an overwhelming threat and turns inward, away from usual support systems. He feels isolated. The negotiator's task is to help the subject return to his normal functioning level.

Crisis Characteristics

In an effort to relieve his overwhelming stress, the subject will engage in all kinds of behavior. Some of it may be impulsive, inappropriate, dangerous, and out of character for him. Attempts to relieve stress can include heavy drinking or drug use, reckless driving, barroom brawls, promiscuous sex, eating binges, and a wide variety of other potentially self-destructive behaviors.

A mental health professional told of a patient who, when stressed, took his car out onto the plains, reached a speed of 120 mph and rolled the automobile. He has performed this "stress relieving" act on three different occasions. According to him, "You can't believe how good it feels to walk away."

People in a crisis state will experience increasingly constricted and narrow thinking. Additionally, they may have a lowered attention span, might not be able to discern between small problems and large ones, and see no way out of their situation. Their intense emotional response to their circumstances will cause a disorganized, shotgun approach to problem-solving.

Once the person has his emotions back under control, it may be beneficial for the negotiator to ask questions such as: What do you think about...? What would happen if...? What would you like to happen? The negotiator should beware, however, of getting into problem-solving before the subject is ready to solve the problem.

Often there will be changes in the subject's social network. He may travel around the country saying good-bye to relatives, attempt to repair old, broken relationships or simply withdraw from his relationships.

Physical problems are also associated with crisis states. It is not unusual, for example, for people to visit a doctor in the days or weeks before a suicide. Unfortunately, mental problems are still viewed as shameful by some people whereas physical problems are not. Perhaps these suicidal individuals are looking for a physical explanation to a mental problem.

In working with a person in a crisis state, the negotiator will not have to wait long for a change. The incident will get better or worse in a relatively short period of time, that is, in a matter of a few hours.

Crisis Intervention

Crisis intervention is a collection of techniques intended to return individuals in crisis to their normal functioning level and to get them past possibly dangerous impulses. Most of the incidents worked by law enforcement negotiators fit this description. Negotiators are present to enforce the law and to preserve life and property. It is not a negotiator's responsibility to provide therapy, change personalities, or solve all the subject's problems in living.

The Purposes of Crisis Intervention

In their basic hostage negotiation course, negotiators are taught that their task is to allow the subject to ventilate, to calm him, stall for time, establish rapport, and gather information of use to the negotiation and tactical teams as well as management. Crisis intervention is how negotiators achieve these objectives. The primary tool of crisis intervention is active listening.

Chapter 4

Active Listening

For negotiators, active listening is the ability to see a circumstance from another's perspective and to let the other person know that the negotiator understands his perspective. Active listening is used by many professions requiring "people" skills and, unfortunately, it is just starting to take hold in law enforcement—especially among crisis negotiators.

Active listening may turn out to be particularly effective when employed by negotiators because so many of the people encountered by negotiators have never had anyone truly listen to what they were saying. When a crisis negotiator sits down to listen to the subject, it is possibly the first time in that man's entire life that anyone listened carefully to what he was saying and seemed to care about what he was feeling. When skillfully applied, active listening can be a powerful tool for crisis negotiators.

Active Listening Assumptions

Chief Justice of the Supreme Court John Marshall (1755-1835) said, "To listen well is as powerful a means of communication and influence as to talk well." Contrary to what some people might suppose, the primary skill of good negotiators is not smooth talking, but practiced listening. An assumption about active listening is that people who clearly understand their feelings are better able to resolve their emotional problems. A second assumption is that when the negotiator demonstrates an understanding of the person's feelings, the negotiator is seen as being empathetic and understanding and that builds rapport.

Active Listening Concepts

The negotiator's objective is to build rapport by demonstrating empathy, understanding, and objectivity, thereby establishing trust and rapport. Sympathy implies pity and over-involvement. If the negotiator gets too involved and shows pity, the individual may feel justified in how he is feeling and lose any confidence in the negotiator's ability to help him.

A common statement by persons in crisis is, "How do you know how I feel? Have you ever ...?"

It is possible to understand another's feelings without going through the same experience because, while experiences are not universal, feelings are. Degrees of feelings are also universal. We have all experienced the same shades of depression, sadness, or the blues, for example. No life is a mirror of another's, but we have all experienced the same feelings and degrees of feeling.

However, do not make any assumptions about a person's feelings based on his circumstances. Many of us know people who were near suicidal over a divorce and many of us also know people who were jubilant over a divorce. A negotiator must not be tempted to make assumptions about how someone else feels based on a similar situation in the negotiator's past.

After a tense 10-hour domestic situation, a subject went out on the front porch and killed himself in front of a crowd of his friends, neighbors, police, and onlookers. The negotiator reported that it would be necessary for the entire negotiation team to be debriefed by the departmental chaplain. The negotiator's position was that she had tried her best, but that the subject had chosen another ending to the incident. She concluded that his emotional reaction to his situation and thus his behavior were his responsibility, not hers.

Despite the above negotiator's healthy assessment of her situation, it is always a good idea to have a mandatory debriefing session. This is especially important in a situation where a death has occurred.

A negotiator can help, but it is important to remember that the subject's actions are his own responsibility and never the negotiator's responsibility. Never take on a responsibility that is the subject's burden.

Sergeant Joe Friday on the old *Dragnet* television program was, in effect, asking for only half of the story when he said, "Just the facts, ma'am. Just the facts."

The sergeant was limiting himself to just half of the story because people communicate on two levels—the simple facts and their emotional reaction to the facts. It is important for the negotiator to focus on the emotional message behind the facts. The facts do not make the situation a crisis, but the emotional reaction and subsequent behavior that can turn a dispute into a tragedy. How a subject feels about a situation will strongly influence what he does. So, controlling the subject's emotions will help control his behavior.

Values are what people think is important and so have a strong influence on behavior. Values not only affect behavior but a person's expectations in any given situation. While at the home of a probationer, a probation officer was asked by the probationer's mother to talk to her youngest son. The officer agreed to talk to the 16 year-old but asked the purpose of the talk. The mother said, "He's 16 years old and the only one of my eight kids who has never been arrested by this age. Something is wrong."

The subject's values and expectations, as well as his family's values and expectations, will often be different from the negotiator's. A young man who was a long-term drug user was holding his ex-girlfriend at gunpoint. During an interview, the subject's mother was asked if her son was currently using drugs. She said, "Oh, no, no. He hasn't used drugs in, oh, two, maybe three weeks."

It might be helpful to clarify the subject's values during an incident. An understanding of his values and what he thinks could help the negotiator know what is going on in his mind. If there is a value conflict going on, that is bound to affect his actions.

The negotiator should maintain a nonjudgmental attitude and be as accepting as possible. No one would expect the negotiator to become friends with the subject or, at the other extreme, to hate him. In some respects, the situation is like anything else in law enforcement, such as stopping a speeder, for example. Officers can dislike everyone they stop, but if that is their attitude, they are not going to last very long. Likewise, negotiators do not inject their feelings, values, and opinions into the situation. The negotiator works with the subject's feelings, values, lifestyles, and opinions.

Active Listening Skills

An important aspect of active listening techniques is that they demonstrate to the subject that the negotiator is listening and "tuned in" to what he or she is being told in terms of facts and emotions. As the old saying goes, "Talk is cheap." It is far more valuable for the negotiator to demonstrate understanding through active listening than to merely say, "I understand."

Emotion Labeling

Certainly, a negotiator listens to the facts, but does not confine his or her interest to that aspect of the situation. It is more important to be attuned to the subject's emotional reaction to the facts, i.e., the emotion behind the words and facts. Commonly, negotiators want to get into problem-solving too early. Too early an approach to problem solving is doomed to failure because the subject is not ready to reason and the negotiator has not listened enough to get all of the information he or she needs to assist in problem solving.

Emotion labeling, then, is the first active listening skill to be used in an incident. The intent of emotion labeling is to respond, not strictly to content, but to the emotions heard in the subject's voice. To emotion label the negotiator uses the following words:

- You sound (emotion heard by the negotiator). Example: You sound angry.
- You seem (emotion heard by the negotiator). Example: You seem hurt.
- I hear (emotion heard by the negotiator). Example: I hear frustration.

Emotion labeling demonstrates that the negotiator is listening and tuned in to the emotions the subject is experiencing. A negotiator does not tell people how they are feeling but how they seem or sound as if they are feeling to the negotiator. A negotiator should not hesitate and should label every emotion heard throughout the incident whenever emotions are expressed.

The negotiator must not be concerned about making a mistake in labeling emotions. If an emotion is incorrectly labeled, the subject will correct the negotiator and will often appear grateful for the attempt.

The presence, absence, and presentation of emotions tell the negotiator a lot about the subject's emotional state or even mental health. Negotiators should be aware of missing emotions and listen for conflicts in the feelings expressed. They should also note when the emotions expressed are inappropriate to the situation described.

At the same time, the subject will be listening to the emotions that are indicated in the negotiator's voice. Voice tone can tell the subject how the negotiator feels about the situation, and can transmit his or her sincerity or, perhaps, trustworthiness.

Emotion labeling is not an appropriate technique when the negotiator is being verbally attacked. For example, if a subject is yelling and screaming at the negotiator, he or she should not say, "You seem angry."

If the negotiator is being verbally attacked, an "I" message is more appropriate. This situation is described later in this chapter.

Paraphrasing

Paraphrasing is a summary in the negotiator's own words of what he or she was just told. It demonstrates that the negotiator is listening, creates empathy, and establishes rapport because it is made evident the negotiator has heard and understood. Paraphrasing usually begins with the words, "Are you telling me (what the negotiator heard)?" or "Are you saying (what the negotiator heard)?"

Paraphrasing has many uses, some of which are as follows:

- It creates empathy and rapport because it is a demonstration that the negotiator has been listening.
- It clarifies content and highlights issues.
- It tends to make the subject a listener.
- It promotes give and take between the subject and negotiator.

- It does not put the subject on the defensive because the words being spoken by the negotiator are his words.
- Hearing his demands spoken aloud for the first time may give the subject a new perspective on them.

Reflecting or Mirroring

Reflecting, or mirroring, is the technique of repeating the last word or phrase the subject said and putting a question mark after it. This technique provides very exact responses because, once again, the negotiator is using the subject's own words.

Reflecting or mirroring asks for more input without guiding the direction of the subject's thoughts and elicits information when the negotiator does not have enough to ask a pertinent question. It is also very useful for those instances where the negotiator is at a loss for words. It also provides an opportunity for the subject to think about what the negotiator has said.

Silence

The negotiator can use silence very effectively for a number of purposes. Most people are not comfortable with silence and will fill it with talk. It is to the negotiator's advantage to keep the subject talking.

In addition to encouraging the subject to talk, silence can be used to emphasize a point. The negotiator can use silence just before or just after saying something important.

Minimal Encouragers

Minimal encouragers is a fancy term for a very simple technique. Minimal encouragers are the sounds made, especially on the telephone, to let one person know the other is there and listening. Generally, they are short questions such as, "Oh?", "When?", and "Really?" They are questions, comments, or sounds that do not interfere with the flow of conversation, but do let the subject know that the negotiator is there and listening. Minimal encouragers are useful because they help build rapport and encourage the subject to continue talking.

"I" Messages

"I" messages enable negotiators to let the subject know how he is making them feel, why they feel that way, and what the subject can do to remedy the situation. It conveys the above information in a non-threatening way and does not put the subject on the defensive. An "I" message is worded this way:

I feel (the emotion the negotiator is feeling) when you (the subject's behavior) because (the negotiator's reason).

During an aircraft hijacking, a subject was using a lot of profanity in his remarks to a female negotiator and the use of his abusive language seemed to be stirring himself up. The negotiator said to the hijacker, "I feel uneasy when you talk like that because I'm not used to men talking like that around me."

After the negotiator used the "I" message, the hijacker immediately eliminated all obscenities and vulgarities. When he stopped using the abusive language, he calmed down.

An "I" message is used when communication is difficult because of the intense emotions being directed at the negotiator. It is also used when the subject is trying to manipulate the negotiator and the negotiator wants him to stop the attempts. Negotiators also use this technique to refocus the subject and when they are being verbally attacked.

Open-Ended Questions

Asking open-ended questions encourages the person to say more without actually directing the conversation. They are questions that cannot be answered with a single word such as "yes" or "no." Open-ended questions get information for the negotiator with fewer questions, those that usually begin with how, what, when, and where.

Notice that "why" questions are generally not asked directly. Questions that begin with "why" tend to steer the conversation toward blame and shut down communication. A subject often cannot answer a "why" question and this makes him feel embarrassed, put on the spot, defensive, and even angry. Anyone with children also knows that "why" questions can always be answered with "because." The primary use of open-ended questions is to help a subject start talking. Whenever he is talking, negotiators are learning more about him.

A closed-end question asks for specific information and can be answered in a word or phrase. Negotiators should avoid asking closed-end questions except for emergency situations when it is necessary to elicit specific information such as assessing the seriousness of a suicide-in-progress. Closed-end questions give a feeling of interrogation that makes rapport building difficult. They also cause the negotiator to work too hard at thinking up new questions.

Chapter 5

Suicide Intervention

Hostage Negotiators and Suicide Intervention

While hostage negotiation and suicide intervention are not the same thing, there is a lot of overlap in terms of the necessity to contain the incident, gather intelligence, set up perimeters, establish contact with the subject, and so on. These points of similarity are covered in the chapter on hostage negotiation.

In the 1970s and early 1980s, it was not as obvious as it is now to law enforcement personnel that hostage negotiators would be asked to work suicide situations. An assumption made by some people was that hostage negotiation and suicide intervention are the same thing. They are not. A trained hostage negotiator is not prepared to properly engage in suicide intervention.

It is important for hostage negotiators to be trained in suicide intervention for many reasons. For example, a chain of events many negotiators have observed over the years is that spontaneous sieges often evolve into barricade situations that then evolve into suicide situations.

Suicide intervention can be very difficult—perhaps even more difficult than hostage negotiation. Some estimate that as many as 5 percent of those who threaten suicide are intent on ending their lives and, in their determination, they will be very difficult, if not impossible, to stop.

The impact on the negotiator of "losing" in a suicide situation can be severe. Through the hours of an incident, they get to know suicidal individuals extremely well. To then have that person commit suicide, perhaps before the negotiator's eyes, can be very traumatic for the negotiator.

An element that might make suicide situations difficult for law enforcement personnel is that many of the persons with whom negotiations are conducted have problems similar to those encountered frequently by law enforcement personnel. Law enforcement officers have high rates of divorce, alcoholism, and stress-related illnesses. In fact, in studies of suicide rate by occupation, law enforcement rates are invariably high. A side benefit to suicide intervention training is that negotiators might see some suicide clues among their colleagues and be in a position to help.

Suicide Clues

Suicidal persons very commonly provide clues to their intent. Sometimes such "clues" are actually statements of purpose as opposed to being mere hints. Unfortunately, too often friends and relatives are not prepared to listen or do not take the clues seriously. Too often, family and friends will insist that he stop talking "that way" or tell him that they don't want to hear "that kind of talk."

Expressions of hopelessness and helplessness are very serious suicide clues and are sometimes seen as the dividing line between depression and the intent to actually go on to commit suicide. Until a depressed person starts feeling that there is no hope of their situation ever getting better and there is no one who can possibly help them they will not be suicidal.

There are other suicide clues such as direct verbal clues, i.e., telling people of their intent. The suicidal person may even travel the country, visiting relatives and saying his farewells. Suicidal people might also furnish indirect verbal clues, i.e., hint at their suicidal intent. Indirect clues sometimes include time clues such as, "You won't have to put up with me much longer."

The subject will possibly make statements to the negotiator such as, "Officer, everything will be all right in just a few minutes."

"Verbal wills" are behavioral clues that include giving away treasured items. Relationship clues may also provide some indication of suicidal intent. Relationship clues include such things as attempting to repair old, broken relationships or withdrawing from relationships. The subject may also travel to visit relatives and friends he has not seen in a while. During these visits he might actually say good-bye and state his suicidal intent.

Determining Suicidal Intent

Determining if someone is suicidal usually is not difficult. Depressed people will often be straightforward and honest with the negotiator. It will likely take courage on the negotiator's part to ask about suicidal intent. People avoid asking about suicidal intent for a variety of reasons, such as the fear of how the subject might respond. No one wants to hear that another person wants to take his or her life.

How to Determine if a Person is Suicidal

Ask: "Are you going to commit suicide?"

Negotiators should ask the above question precisely as written. They should not ask, "Are you going to hurt yourself?" or something similar. Negotiators should not attempt to skirt the question but confront the problem directly. Depressed and suicidal persons will take a negotiator literally. Because the negotiator is an authority figure, any statement that sounds like permission to commit suicide might be acted upon. Also, the subject does not intend to "hurt" himself. He intends to kill himself.

The willingness of the negotiator to discuss suicidal intent will help establish rapport with the subject because suicidal individuals have often told others of their intent and they were not taken seriously. In fact, family and friends may have told him not to talk that way and belittled his problems.

Asking directly about suicidal intent is not going to put the idea into someone's mind. A negotiator cannot implant the idea of suicide in the mind of a healthy individual. No well-balanced human being will ever say, "Good idea, officer," and proceed to kill himself.

The negotiator will suspect that the individual is suicidal and the subject knows he is suicidal. Asking directly puts the issue up front for discussion. A problem cannot be solved until it is confronted directly.

Potential High-Risk Indicators

The number of "high-risk" indicators provides a measurement of the seriousness of all suicide threats. Negotiators should take *all* suicide threats seriously.

Hopelessness and Helplessness

The feelings of hopelessness and helplessness can be viewed as the emotions that separate the merely depressed from the truly suicidal.

History of Impulsivity

Any indications of impulsivity in the subject's past are not good signs. To determine if a subject is impulsive, negotiators should check "wants and warrants" and his arrest record. If his arrest record indicates multiple speeding citations, numerous parking tickets, or arrests for assault, he should be considered impulsive. Additionally, persons who know the subject well will report that the subject does not like people "getting in his face" or that he lashes out quickly—verbally and physically—at others.

People may think or fantasize about suicide for long periods of time but the act itself is considered an impulsive one. To preclude an impulsive suicidal act, the negotiator should verbally "stay with" the subject as much as possible.

Family History of Suicide

While there is no suicide gene, the propensity to commit suicide does recur in families. Perhaps, if another family member has committed suicide, the taboo has been removed. Or, a family may talk in reverential terms about "Grandpa," who killed himself years ago, and the subject wants the family to remember him that way.

Margaux Hemingway, at the age of 41, killed herself with an overdose of barbiturates on July 1, 1996. That date was the anniversary her famous grandfather, Ernest Hemingway, had killed himself with a shotgun in 1961. His brother, sister, and father also killed themselves. (Benzodiazepine tranquilizers have, to a significant extent, displaced barbiturates because they have a higher lethal dosage.)

Suicide Intervention 29

In a lesser-known case, an officer reported that a man commemorated the anniversary of his brother's suicide by committing the same act himself. Both brothers hanged themselves by jumping off the back of the same pickup truck with a rope thrown over the same limb of the same tree.

Test-Firing a Weapon

Test-firing a weapon before turning it on themselves is an event suicidal subjects have made familiar to experienced negotiators. He may fire a shot or shots into the wall, the ceiling, or a picture.

Sometimes suicidal individuals "test" shoot or cut themselves in a non-vital area in an apparent attempt to determine how it feels. Negotiators have also been present when suicidal persons inflicted multiple nonlethal wounds upon themselves. As incredible as it may seem, individuals have shot themselves multiple times with a crossbow. To the amazement of onlooking officers, one individual in a very tenacious suicide attempt shot himself 11 times with a 9mm pistol.

Hesitation marks, sometimes called "chicken scratches" by prison inmates, are the multiple cuts left by suicidal individuals before cutting themselves deeply and finally. Perhaps, individuals who test-shoot themselves are performing the firearm equivalent of hesitation marks.

Finding the Person in an Isolated Location

Finding the suicidal individual in an isolated location indicates that they did not want to be interrupted in their attempt. They might go into a nearby forest, to the beach, or a hotel room in a city not far from home. Taking an overdose at home many hours before anyone is due home might also be considered an example of isolating oneself.

The Presence of Drugs and/or Alcohol

The use of drugs or alcohol clouds judgment and rational decision-making and therefore heightens the potential for a violent end.

A Detailed Suicidal Threat, Fantasy, or Plan

People often make vague suicide threats. While not dismissing any suicide threat, the negotiator should be particularly concerned about a threat, fantasy, or plan with a lot of detail. This may indicate that the person has thought about suicide for a long time and now has a relatively fixed plan. In fact, if the negotiator can disrupt the suicidal person's plan, that might be enough to stop the attempt.

Extreme Insomnia

Depressed persons often have no problem getting to sleep but then wake up between the hours of 2:00 a.m. and 5:00 a.m. and cannot get back to sleep. This phenomenon is called "terminal insomnia," meaning toward the end of the night, or "early morning awakening." There appears to be a connection between the degree of insomnia and the degree of suicidal intent. Severe insomnia seems to indicate a higher potential for suicide.

An Experienced Team's "Gut" Feeling

If the negotiator is fortunate enough to be working on an experienced negotiation team and everyone has a bad "gut" feeling about what is going on, the team should not readily dismiss this feeling. The combined experience of the team members will often allow them to sense more going on than might actually be said or acted out.

Increasingly Dangerous Suicidal Gestures

Having a history of past suicide attempts by itself is a bad sign. However, if the past attempts have grown increasingly dangerous, this escalation is an even worse indicator. Depressed persons sometimes "work up" to a lethal attempt.

A Psychological History

Persons with a psychological history, particularly hospitalization, are at high risk. Be wary when family and friends arrive on the scene and tell the negotiation team that your subject was bad a week or two ago but everyone thought he was getting better. They may be right. The subject is not as depressed as he was a week or two ago.

During the insidious slip into a depressive episode he was not suicidal. While in the depths of the depression he did not have the energy to act, but now that he is better he has the energy to take steps toward completing the planned suicide.

Reassurance from the Subject

If the subject begins reassuring the negotiator and the negotiator cannot tie this "improvement" in the situation to anything that the negotiator has said or done, this disclosure is not good. Suicidal persons often have a difficult time making the decision to proceed with the suicide. When the decision is made, the negotiator will hear a change in the subject's voice tone or in what he is saying. He might say something like, "Officer, everything is going to be okay. Just give me a few more minutes."

A negotiator should immediately follow up on such a statement. The negotiator should quickly find out what is happening, as suicidal persons have committed suicide immediately after making "reassurances" to the negotiator. Perhaps the reason the subject is reassuring the netotiator is that he wants the negotiator "off his back" for a few minutes—for whatever reason.

In one case, a deputy was sent to a disturbance call. She entered the residence to discover a suicidal man with a gun to his head. After trying to work with him for an hour and a half, the man reassured her and, seeming to be in the act of putting the gun down, he looked at her, smiled, and shot himself through the head. Other negotiators have been so convinced that the subject was actually giving up his idea and coming out, they believed that, when the subject finally killed himself, it was an accident.

Perhaps the shooting was accidental, and that brings us to the next point. When working with persons not totally familiar with firearms, negotiators should be careful about the instructions provided. It might be best, for example, to tell subjects to put the gun down gently, as opposed to decocking it. It would be very easy for people inexperienced in handling firearms to accidentally shoot themselves with loaded, cocked guns that negotiators had asked them to decock.

Strange Stories and the Role of Fate

Law enforcement officers commonly report stories that reflect the astonishing role of fate and the incredible determination on the part of suicidal persons. A negotiator tells the story of a suicidal individual who attempted to kill himself with a shotgun but succeeded only in blowing his jaw off. The subject then went into his garage and attempted carbon monoxide poisoning but his jaw was hurting so much that he could not wait to die. He then drove his car out to the local gravel pit, set his car on fire and drove off a 45-foot cliff into the gravel pit. The blazing car landed in the pit, rolled and flipped onto its roof. The man got out and walked three blocks looking for help. He had a difficult time finding help, however, because it was Halloween and people were alternately frightened and impressed with his terrible "costume." He has received extensive plastic surgery and, to this day, is still alive.

Another suicidal individual attempted to shoot himself in the temple but only succeeded in blowing his eye out. He was confined to a hospital for a period of time. Upon his return home, he attempted carbon monoxide poisoning in his garage but, upon passing out, fell forward, depressing the garage door opener. The garage door opened, let in fresh air, and saved him. He again spent some time in the hospital. On the third occasion, he threw a rope over a rafter in his garage but when he attempted to hang himself, he pulled the garage roof down on himself. This time, he received quality assistance in the form of couseling during his hospital stay and acquired a new desire to live. Sadly, shortly after his release from the hospital, he was walking across his front lawn to get his mail when a drunk driver drove across his yard and killed him.

A patrol officer, who happened to be a negotiator, was attempting to talk a suicidal man down off of a bridge. The man said that he was afraid the officer would shoot him if he came down and asked that the officer put his weapon on the roadbed. With some reluctance and trepidation, the officer took his weapon out of his holster, put it on the roadbed, and placed his foot on it. When the subject was three feet above the officer's head, he jumped, knocking the officer to the ground. The subject then picked up the officer's gun and, at point-blank range, pulled the trigger. The gun misfired and the accompanying tactical team killed the subject. The patrol officer said that his weapon had never misfired before and has not misfired since.

Deputies were sent on a "disturbance" call without details as to the disturbance. As they were milling around attempting to determine what was happening, they heard a clicking sound. When they asked a nearby man to turn around, they saw that he was holding a revolver under his chin. The deputies disarmed him, only to find he had pulled the trigger six times. Six rounds had "dimples" in the primer. The next day, the weapon and ammunition were taken out to the departmental range for a test firing. This time, all six rounds were fired from the same gun without a failure.

Suicide as a Problem-Solving Option

Negotiators tend to view a particular suicide threat as a problem, while the suicidal person sees suicide as the ultimate solution to his problem. The suicide becomes a means of coping with a problem and is intended to deal with and solve a problem. So, suicide becomes a goal-oriented coping method.

Suicidal persons often feel as if they have lost control of events in their lives and the act of suicide becomes a means of regaining control. Suicide also becomes a kind of revenge. The suicidal person may be thinking, "I can't wait to see the look on my husband's face when he comes home and finds me dead."

Or, "I'll swerve my car into this oncoming 18-wheeler. That will show her. She'll be sorry."

Communicating Suicidal Intent

Communicating the intent to commit suicide is not uncommon. There are perhaps as many reasons as there are suicidal persons. Some suicidal persons travel the country visiting relatives and overtly saying good-bye. Perhaps this trip is a final effort to find some hope or help in their situation.

Some people have a fear of dying alone. This fear and the need to communicate to someone how much pain they are experiencing possibly accounts for a relatively common phenomenon seen by experienced negotiators. Often a barricaded subject will come out of his house onto the front porch to kill himself in front of friends, relatives, neighbors, and police.

When working a barricade situation, one can never assume that a suicidal person is alone. In fact, it may be a good idea to assume that there is one more subject than is seen or heard.

Some suicidal persons look for someone to say that dying is the right and appropriate thing to do. In effect, they are not only looking for someone to say that it is right, but are looking for someone to give them permission to proceed. Depressed and suicidal individuals often will take a negotiator's words literally. A negotiator, who at that moment is an authority figure, should take special care to avoid any language that sounds as if he or she is giving permission to commit suicide or agrees with the subject's suicidal intent.

A patrol officer encountered a young man armed with a rifle and threatening suicide over a broken romance. The young man asked to see his parish priest and his request was granted. The subject was expressing a great deal of ambivalence about living and dying and, at the same time, the officer and priest were attempting to have him put his rifle down. The priest said, "Go ahead and do it my son."

The subject replied, "Yes, Father," and proceeded to blow the top of his head off. The priest had meant that the subject should put the rifle down, but that is not the way the young man took his comment. Again, negotiators must be careful about how they word things, as depressed individuals could take their words literally and act upon them with tragic results.

Basic Concepts for Crisis Negotiators

Negotiators will try to stop all suicidal persons. Although they are rarely fully informed as to the facts of a particular person's circumstances, and there may even be facts the subject does not know or is not clear on, negotiators must make no judgments as to whether a suicide is justified.

A suicidal person may put the negotiator in crisis. A significant percentage of the general population, and law enforcement in particular, have viewed suicide at least as a fleeting option at some point in their lives. Negotiators must be wary of being emotionally drawn into an incident and endangering their own lives or the lives of others.

All suicidal persons are volatile and emotionally unstable in the extreme and the situation can change violently in a split second.

Negotiators must also assume that suicidal persons are dangerous and will hurt someone if given the opportunity. There have been at least 25 law enforcement officers killed while acting as negotiators. Suicidal persons killed all of these individuals, so law enforcement officers should assume that anyone exposed to the line of fire could be killed or wounded. Never presuppose that suicidal persons are dangerous to themselves alone.

Negotiators must take all suicide threats seriously. A negotiator cannot afford to assume that a particular suicide threat is merely gestural or a cry for attention. Nor should one assume that a particular social, sexual, religious, ethnic, or economic group is immune to suicide. Various societal groups have varying rates but no group is immune.

The negotiator may assume that every suicidal person has some ambivalence. As negotiators we must take for granted that the suicidal person is experiencing at least some doubts about going through with the suicide. If he was 100 percent committed to the idea, he would have done it before negotiators arrived.

Why Commit Suicide?

The primary reasons people commit suicide are hopelessness and helplessness. They feel there is no hope of their situation improving and that no one can help them. Losses, especially sudden losses, are often associated with depression and suicide.

The elderly white population in the United States has a particularly high suicide rate. When one looks at the reasons that these people commit suicide it becomes more evident why their suicide rates are high. Often these elderly folks have moved to the warm south, leaving their children and grandchildren "up north." Their offspring, now with kids of their own, telephone and visit less and less and the elderly become increasingly isolated. The elderly begin experiencing losses in terms of the death of spouses, siblings, and friends and, of course, their own parents have long since died. All of these losses lead to feelings of social isolation and acute loneliness, and they begin to feel all alone in the world.

Often the elderly are suffering from chronic illness and pain and do not want to be a burden to their family. Their lifestyle is no longer at the level it once was and they never envisioned their senior years to be this way. They kill themselves at a high rate.

Determine Motivation

Negotiators should attempt to determine the motivation for the suicide threat. Why does the suicidal individual want to die? What does the person want to achieve? The negotiator should ask, "Do you really want to die or do you want to hurt or get even with someone?"

Often the suicidal person's motivation or goal is to stop the flow of consciousness, not death. Commonly, however, such people are suffering from an unendurable level of psychological pain or stress that is pushing them toward suicide.

Ambivalence

Ambivalence is a common internal attitude. The suicidal individual has an inner conflict between the desire to live and the pain of living. Negotiators might say, for example, "You say you want to die, but I hear in your voice a part of you that really wants to live." Assuming that ambivalence is present, the negotiator may want to say the aforementioned sentence even when they do not hear the ambivalence.

Anger

Though not all depression is an outgrowth of unexpressed anger, negotiators should assume for their personal safety and the safety of others that the subject is angry. In fact, the negotiator may not be able to resolve some incidents involving unexpressed anger until the subject gets angry at least once. It would be wise, therefore, to emotion-label anger when it arises and let the subject vent his anger.

This does not mean to suggest that the negotiator should deliberately make the subject angry. The negotiator's objective is to vent the anger that is already present, not make the subject even more angry.

Suicide-By-Cop

In one instance, an officer made what he thought was going to be a routine traffic stop. The driver, who was an enormous man, exited the car and charged at the officer raging, "Kill me. Kill me. You're going to have to kill me or I'll kill you."

The officer, not knowing what to do with this giant unarmed man, started backing up. He soon found himself in a footrace around and around the patrol car with the citizen in hot pursuit and bent on doing violence to someone. While running around his patrol car, the officer excitedly radioed for back up. The incident did not end until the man became winded and help at last arrived. This incident took place in the early 1980s before suicide-by-cop became the widely known phenomenon it is today.

Suicide-by-cop refers to a suicide where the person wants to die but prefers to have the police kill him as opposed to killing himself. There are perhaps more of these impulsive incidents than most law enforcement officials imagine. In some respects, they are like the disguised suicides of people running off the road on a clear night or the "accidental" discharge of a weapon. These suicides may be disguised or overt.

There are several possible indicators of suicide-by-cop. Some are obvious and some are less so. Listed below are some of the indicators seen by law enforcement:

- There is nothing subtle about this indicator in that the subject may demand or challenge the officer or agency to kill him.
- He may set a deadline for his own death. The deadline may be "right now" or 30 minutes from now.
- Often, some traumatic, precipitating event has happened in the recent past. "Recent past" means within the hour to a couple of days.

Any time the negotiator hears talk of suicide, he or she should assume that the subject means what he says. Talk of suicide includes such things as a "verbal will." In a verbal will, the subject asks the negotiator to make sure that some of his possessions get to the intended recipient. For example, a 16 year-old boy may ask that his 14 year-old sister get his collection of CDs.

The suicide plan can be impulsive or elaborate. Detail in a suicide threat, plan, or fantasy is always a factor that should cause concern. In an impulsive suicide-by-cop, the negotiator is not likely to be on scene because the deed has been done before he is able to get there.

The individual who commits suicide-by-cop is likely to be an impulsive person. As such, a check with the departmental records division will often reveal arrests for past assaultive behavior, multiple speeding citations, disturbing the peace, outstanding parking tickets, and other indicators of impulsivity. Some people may consider the killing of oneself to be somewhat less than manly. The individual intent on suicide-by-cop is looking for a "manly" way to commit suicide.

Any time a negotiator hears expressions of hopelessness and helplessness, he or she should be thinking about the possibility of suicide.

In another twist on this type of suicide, the subject might indicate that he wants to "go out big," and certainly killing a cop would be going out big. Negotiators must be alert to the possibility of this plan and never allow a situation to develop to the point where the subject has an opportunity to kill an officer in an effort to provoke other officers into killing him.

If killing a cop is going out big, killing the chief or sheriff would be going out even bigger. Negotiators should beware when a subject says he will surrender only to the chief or sheriff.

When a man loses his job, he has the support of his family to fall back on. Or, when a man loses his family through death, desertion, or divorce, he has the support of the people he works with to fall back on. When a man loses both his job and family over a short period of time, he has lost his two primary sources of support and does not have much left. Some experienced negotiators refer to this situation as the "double whammy" and often find they are talking to individuals who have broken down as a result of this experience.

An individual contemplating suicide-by-cop may refuse to talk to the negotiator. He may be refusing to talk because his mind is made up and there is nothing left to talk about.

The suicidal individual might arrange a dangerous situation for the police and/or hostages. He might try to arrange circumstances so that the police will have little option but to kill him.

This suicidal individual could also escalate the situation until the police must take tactical action to stop him. The escalation may be in the form of homicidal threats, shots being fired, movement toward the police with his weapon pointed at them, or other dangerous actions. This escalation in the incident will be in clear-cut, well-defined steps.

Persons committing suicide-by-cop often will have demonstrated prior suicidal behavior. Always, when working with suicidal individuals, use extreme caution, as they may attempt to kill a hostage, citizen, or officer in order to provoke them into killing him. If the negotiator is in doubt about the subject's suicidal intent, again, ask, "Are you going to commit suicide?"

This time, he may come back to the negotiator and say, "No. I'm not going to kill myself. You guys are going to kill me."

Indicators of Progress in Suicide Situations

Unfortunately, there may be no reliable indicators of negotiation progress in a suicide case. Even worse, what appears to be progress may be just the opposite. However, having said there may be no reliable indicators, there are a few signs that would not be considered bad signs. For example, if the subject is talking at all to the negotiator, that is solid sign of ambivalence. If the negotiator and subject can find a least one reason for the subject to live, progress is being made. If the subject has made any concessions, but especially concessions that reduce lethality, such as putting the gun down, perhaps progress is being made.

Calling a "Time Out" in Suicide Situations

Unlike hostage and barricade situations, where subjects may sometimes be left to think over their situation for relatively long periods of time, negotiators should never take a "time out" while working suicides. The negotiator should stay with the subject at all times, if at all practical. If the negotiator, the subject's final hope, is face-to-face, as with a jumper, do not leave him alone. If the negotiator were to leave, the jumper might see that as the departure of his final hope.

Exposed Face-To-Face In Suicide Situations

Negotiators are strongly urged to not go face-to-face with someone holding an edged weapon, a firearm, or a bomb. If negotiators or officers find themselves in that situation, retreat. Officers should seek adequate cover and negotiate from the new position. Use extreme caution.

If face-to-face with a jumper, give him a lot of space. A natural tendency when falling is to grab for something to hold onto. Negotiators should be wary of jumpers accidentally—or intentionally—pulling the negotiator off a bridge or tall building with them.

Crisis Intervention Techniques

- Negotiators should explore the person's feelings continually using active listening techniques, particularly emotion-labeling.
- Allow the subject to vent feelings, and focus on getting the person to express his feelings.
- Let the person get angry. The expression of anger can be viewed as a positive development in many suicide situations. Anger is often present. Its expression and venting could be the first indication of a resolution.
- Focus on the cause of suicidal feelings. The negotiator should ask, "What has happened to cause you to feel this way?" Often, some incident has occurred within the last day or two to bring about the suicidal action.

Talk openly, even vividly, about the finality of death. Many suicidal people have an unrealistic, rather "romantic" view of suicide. It is acceptable to talk about the reality of suicide. Remind a woman who is trying to make her husband sorry that she will not be there to see the look on her husband's face when he finds her dead. Remind her how messy a suicide really is. The reality of suicide is not romantic by anyone's standards.

One negotiator, when confronted by a man intending to kill himself with a firearm, suggested that a gunshot to the head was extremely messy and particularly unpleasant. The suicidal man then said that he would hang himself in the garage. The negotiator told the man he had seen someone who had hanged himself and that death, too, was ugly. The negotiator said that the man's neck had stretched to what seemed an impossible length and that in hanging himself he had lost control of his bowels and soiled his clothes. The suicidal man then said he would go into the garage, turn on the car and kill himself with carbon monoxide. The negotiator followed that idea with, "Well, you could do that, too. I saw a man who did that and what surprised me was the odd color of his skin and how fast the body had started decomposing. It was really terrible."

The suicidal man then said, "Aw, the hell with it! The hell with it!" He was later taken into custody and received help.

Focus on the specific situation that caused the person to feel suicidal. The incident might seem small to the negotiator but it is not to the suicidal person. So, do not dismiss any event because it seems relatively inconsequential.

The negotiator should have the person describe the suicide as fantasized. If negotiators can disrupt the plan or fantasy, they have a better chance of resolving the incident without a suicide. If the suicide plan is disrupted, it is unlikely that the suicidal person will abruptly come up with a new plan.

Explore what is still meaningful to the suicidal person. Some negotiators call this meaningful theme the "hook." After the hook is determined, negotiators should keep returning to it throughout the incident.

An intervention team opened negotiations with an elderly man who was terminally ill and intending to shoot himself. His wife had left him. He had sold his house and put the proceeds into a trust fund for his son. He had called relatives to say good-bye. Negotiators took the "romance" out of the suicide by explaining that shooting oneself was a particularly nasty way to die and that his daughters would be required to clean up afterward. The subject's only remaining interest seemed to be restoring old cars. A negotiator finally talked the man out of the house by offering him an old car that the negotiator owned and no longer wanted.

In one southern state, officers used what might be considered the opposite of the hook. It was 3:00 a.m. and they were negotiating with an armed young man on LSD who was standing in the middle of a pond. It was cold and the young man was becoming hypothermic. Upon learning that the subject had a strong aversion to alligators, a log was tossed into the water out of his sight. Officers yelled, "Gator," and the young man hastily exited the pond and was arrested.

Negotiators should stall for time in any way they possibly can. Negotiators want the subject's impulse to commit suicide to pass.

Help the suicidal individual put his or her actions into perspective. Discussing what the subject actually hopes to achieve by committing suicide will help achieve this negotiation objective.

The suicidal person may not see all of his options; stress that suicide is only one of many alternatives. Help the subject find additional alternatives and perhaps even list the alternatives in terms of acceptability. It is certainly possible that the subject might see all of his alternatives as unacceptable. If so, help him to determine the least objectionable and work on that option.

Intertwined among his options, the person fears something worse than death—being left alone, endless pain, the situation worsening, etc. The option to die is desirable because they view death as tranquil, peaceful, and comfortable.

Last,, the negotiator ought to express his or her personal concern. Be prepared for the subject to accuse the negotiator of being paid to express concern. Negotiators should assure the suicidal individual that they are negotiating not because they are paid to do so, but that they are volunteers who care about people and want to help.

Negotiator Qualities

- First and foremost, negotiators should be nonjudgmental. They must be prepared for the fact that the suicidal individual's lifestyle is not going to be the negotiator's lifestyle.
- Crisis- and suicide intervention are not therapy. Law enforcement negotiators have the limited goal of getting the person past the impulse to commit suicide. Negotiators should not attempt to be analytical, as this is not their goal or expertise.
- Avoid lecturing, as persons in crisis need support, not a speech.
- Do not make statements that discount the person's feelings such as, "It's not that bad." To the suicidal person, it is that bad. If negotiators say it is not, they are making it very obvious that they do not understand.
- Negotiators need to avoid moralizing. Like his values, the subject's morals are not going to be the same as theirs.
- Likewise, avoid giving advice. The negotiator's task is to help the person find his or her own solution.

Chapter 6

Hostage Negotiation

Presented in this chapter are what have now become traditional hostage negotiation techniques, theories, and procedures.

Priorities

The number one priority in crisis negotiation is the preservation of human life, any life. Everything else is secondary. A human life cannot be replaced. Our frustration, overtime budget, manpower concerns, inconvenience to the city, boredom, values, embarrassment and anger should play no part in crisis management's decision to take a life or risk the lives of their officers, even if those officers are willing to risk their lives. Law enforcement crisis managers make the decision to take tactical action because they *must* do so—not merely because they can.

Courses of Action

The authorities can initiate any number of actions in siege situations. The course advocated here is contain, isolate, and negotiate. The negotiator wants the subject contained in the smallest possible area and isolated from the outside world. The subject is isolated in that he has no dialogue with anyone outside the siege location unless the crisis management team agrees to that contact.

The tactical options are varied and include chemical agents, sniper shots, and an assortment of entry alternatives. The difficulty with all tactical options is that, once initiated, generally they must carried through to completion. If the tactical option fails to end an incident, it can be difficult to initiate or restore negotiations.

Containment

Containment is essential to the resolution of an incident. Containment presupposes that the incident is not moving. Therefore, if the incident is moving, the subject is not contained, and a very dangerous situation exists.

Containment not only prevents escape and spread of the threat, it also prevents the entry of unauthorized persons into the operational area. Unauthorized persons include the subject's supporters, media representatives, and the public and thereby supports the negotiator's need to isolate the subject from the outside world. Containment also prevents injury to these same individuals.

Perimeters

Solid perimeters are essential to containment. The subject is contained within an inner perimeter. The doctrine of most law enforcement agencies is that the tactical team leader is the ultimate authority on the inner perimeter. No one is allowed inside, on, or through the inner perimeter unless the tactical team leader approves. This authority extends over the negotiator. If the tactical team leader does not approve the negotiator's presence on the inner perimeter, the negotiator is not allowed on the inner perimeter.

Negotiators who are on the inner perimeter should maintain a position of cover and at least the same level of safety as tactical officers. Any time the negotiator is on the inner perimeter, he or she should be wearing body armor. Negotiators without body armor should not be allowed on the inner perimeter.

Only authorized persons are permitted through the outer perimeter. Specifically who is authorized may be a matter of judgment, departmental policy, and the circumstances of the incident. For example, some agencies routinely establish a media briefing point at a location between the inner and outer perimeters.

A potential problem is keeping the officers who are manning the outer perimeter involved. Too often, they feel left out of the action and under-involved. The crisis-management team must ensure that the outer perimeter does not break down. The problem of unauthorized persons such as friends and relatives of victims and subject, sightseers, and others breaching the outer perimeter for their own reasons is but just one problem.

One agency reported that officers stopped an individual who was talking on a cellular telephone as he was crossing the outer perimeter. It turned out to be the subject talking to the negotiator. He had somehow gotten through the inner perimeter and came close to making his escape through the outer perimeter.

Another agency negotiated the release of a hostage. When the negotiator told the subject it was time to release the hostage, the bad guy said, "She's already gone." The released hostage had passed undetected through the inner and outer perimeters and went home. She had had a tough day.

Obviously, roads that cut through the inner and outer perimeters should be closed and all traffic stopped. Early in an incident, the address for a staging area or command post location must be broadcast. Ensure that responding officers, including negotiators, tactical personnel, and commanders do not pull up in front of the subject's position and into the line of fire.

What Is Negotiable and What Is Not

Generally, food, drink, cigarettes, and other comfort items have been considered negotiable, though alcoholic drinks have been considered non-negotiable by many negotiation teams. Media coverage, too, has been considered negotiable, especially for people with a cause of any kind. Often, schizophrenics and others with grandiose ideas or delusions want to get their message out to the world. Or, persons who have felt wronged by the government or an employer may want to tell the world about their grievance.

Negotiators should attempt to remain flexible—even creative—concerning what is negotiable. Negotiators should view anything that the subject feels is a problem, obstacle, or annoyance as an opportunity for some creative trading. In the course of a bank robbery gone wrong, the veteran bank robber took several hostages. Among his hostages was an elderly man with a bad heart who thought he was having a heart attack and was loudly expressing his concern to the hostage taker. Another hostage began to menstruate during the prolonged siege. She had no sanitary aids with her so she was crying, humiliated, and upset. The negotiator offered the veteran bank robber a deal by saying, "If you send the old man out, I'll send a box of sanitary aids in."

The bank robber replied, "You have a deal, pal," the trade was made, and the elderly man freed.

Drugging food or drink has been consistently considered too dangerous for hostages or the subject. A drug that will knock out the subject rapidly and yet result in no side effects on anyone, regardless of medical condition or age, probably does not exist.

Another concern among law enforcement personnel has been that the hostage taker might give the drugged food or drink to the hostages and wait to see what happens. If the hostages begin to slump to the floor, out cold, the hostage taker is going to suspect something is amiss and the negotiator will lose credibility. So, as a practical matter and for the safety of all, drugged food and drink have not been provided to hostage takers.

The biggest concern about providing drugs and alcohol to the subject appears to be the fear of potential lawsuits rather than practical concerns. For example, a heroin addict is probably more dangerous in withdrawal than while actively under the influence and "nodding out." A heroin addict in withdrawal is agitated, irritable, and aggressive. Few, if any, agencies, however, are willing to take the risk of providing an illicit drug.

Meanwhile, some agencies have very quietly, on rare occasions, supplied alcohol and thus far experienced no problems in doing so. Providing alcohol, though, is a risky proposition. The universal concern is the possibility that the subject will take violent action against someone after law enforcement gave him alcohol. If alcohol is going to be given to a subject, it should at least be determined how alcohol affects him. If he is a pleasant drunk, the risk would appear to be less than if he is nasty while under the influence.

Transportation is generally considered negotiable only if the threat to hostages appears to be increasing, and leaving the siege location is to the tactical advantage of the authorities. The movement of the situation means the dismantling of the inner and, sometimes, the outer perimeter and the rapid reestablishment of these perimeters at a second location.

Historically, the primary problems associated with moving situations have been centered on command, communication, or control. Command problems have been encountered as the moving hostage situation traveled through different jurisdictions. The policy of each jurisdiction, the training level of crisis management personnel, the experience of each crisis management team, the attitude of personnel, the politics of elected officials or other problems associated with public safety and traffic are all constantly changing as the situation moves from one location to another.

Communications are always a problem in crisis situations but are even more so as a crisis situation moves about and crosses from one jurisdiction to another. Even with a common channel among agencies, problems, questions, uncertainties, misunderstandings, and doubts arise. Chaos is virtually unavoidable.

Finally, a certain loss of control is unavoidable in moving incidents. A basic rule of thumb in crisis management is to avoid any action that reduces law enforcement control of an incident. Movement of an incident certainly reduces control.

Historically, giving a hostage taker weapons or ammunition has been considered non-negotiable. The concern is that if the subject does kill someone, law enforcement does not want the killing to take place with a weapon they provided. Even the provision of a malfunctioning weapon has been avoided. The concern is that the hostage taker may test-fire the weapon, determine that it is useless, and lose any trust he might have developed in the negotiator.

The exchange of hostages has also been considered non-negotiable. Trading a law enforcement officer for a hostage has been considered to be especially dangerous. The fear is that the murder of an officer is more notable in some circles than the killing of a citizen so the subject may be more willing to kill an officer.

The subject will rightly consider an officer or deputy to be more of a threat than a citizen and that also heightens the danger to officers who are exchanged. Stress is typically high during a hostage incident but if the hostage is now an officer, the stress and tension are raised even more.

If the subject specifically requests an individual, negotiators must ask themselves why the subject wants that particular person. The negotiator certainly does not want to be responsible for sending someone into a siege location to his or her death. Hostage takers have also been known to use the trade as a ploy to obtain additional hostages. There was a situation in the Midwest where a subject was initially holding one hostage. The subject kept promising to come out if one more family member, one more friend, one more attorney, and so on, were sent in; he eventually surrendered with his eight hostages.

Finally, negotiators do not want to provide an audience for a vindictive suicide. On two occasions on opposite sides of the world, subjects were found holding large knives to their abdomens. Both demanded that estranged loved ones be brought to the scene. When the loved ones did not appear on the subjects' deadlines, they cut themselves. Police immediately produced a wife in one location and an ex-girlfriend in the other. When the subjects saw their respective ladies, each said, "Look what you've done to me," and sliced open their abdomens. As negotiators, we should be asking ourselves if we are playing into the subject's hands and setting up the very suicide situation he planned from the outset.

As a general rule, anyone who comes out of a siege location stays out. No one should be allowed to go back into a crisis situation once they are out and no new person should be allowed to go in. Not uncommonly, people may want to go back into the crisis incident. The general feeling among these people is that they can do more good inside than out. On one occasion, a rather elderly mental health professional had to be removed from the scene because once out of the hostage situation he insisted on going back in with his fellow hostages. In another incident, a minister once out of captivity went back in twice before being sent away from the incident. A somewhat related situation is one where an agreement to release a hostage is reached with the hostage taker and the hostage refuses to come out.

Suggested Negotiator Introduction

Negotiators should establish contact with the subject as soon as possible with consideration given to safety, control, departmental policy, and procedure. Some law enforcement agencies have a policy of not opening a dialogue with the subject until the tactical team is in place. If responding officers are adequately trained, the incident is contained, and innocent people are out of harm's way, this procedure would seem to err on the side of caution. First response training for patrol officers and road deputies should be an important issue for all law enforcement agencies.

Historically, the early hours of an incident have been considered the most dangerous and, for negotiators, the most difficult. It is essential to get the negotiation process off to the best possible start. A good way to begin is by using the following introduction:

"My name is (no rank or title). I am a negotiator with the Police Department. I would like to help."

It is suggested that the negotiator's full name be provided initially but only the first name be used thereafter in an effort to establish a less formal, rapport-building atmosphere. Negotiators give no rank or title to avoid the idea that they have more power than they actually do have. Negotiators, being officers or deputies, have access to the power and it is this access to power, not actual power, that the negotiator projects.

Even using the word "negotiator" has been the topic of some discussion. In the late 1970s and early 1980s, some officers thought that someone called negotiator might be thought of as being manipulative, so the word was dropped from any introduction. Time, as it so often is, has been on the side of negotiators. As criminals became informed about negotiation, some negotiators so designated themselves when working with what appeared to be career criminals. Now, even the general public knows what negotiators do, so the word "negotiator" is back in the introduction.

A negotiator arrived at the scene a couple of hours into at an incident. In his absence, a tactical team member was assuming the negotiator's role. When the officer introduced himself and identifying himself as a negotiator, the subject asked, "You're a negotiator?"

The negotiator said that he was a negotiator. The subject then declared, "Good. I give up."

The incredulous negotiator replied with, "Fine, but why?"

The subject said, "Well, the other guy I was talking to is on the S.W.A.T. team. S.W.A.T. teams kill people. Negotiators talk to people. I give up."

Sometimes, subjects are very grateful to negotiators for having saved their lives. Some negotiators receive notes and even gifts through the mail months—even years—after the incident.

One subject telephoned a negotiator at home in the early morning hours and asked if the negotiator remembered him. The negotiator assured the subject that he did, in fact, remember. The subject then said, "Good, because I've taken a hostage again. I'm down here in a phone booth with the hostage and I wish you would come down and talk me out of this."

When the subject tells the negotiator his name, the negotiator should listen very carefully, make a note of the subject's name and use the name exactly as furnished. If the subject says his name is William, for example, the negotiator should not call him Bill or Billy. The name to use is William. If the negotiator wants to use a more familiar form of a name, he or she should ask the subject how he wants to be addressed.

Getting the name exactly correct may seem like a small point, but from the perspective of experienced negotiators, it is not. Subjects seem to get very upset if the negotiator forgets their name or gets it wrong, or uses a chummy or disrespectful form of a name.

If the subject does not provide a name, the negotiator should work with him and tell him, "I have to call you something. Give me a name, any name, to call you." Even under these circumstances, subjects have become extremely upset when a negotiator got the assigned name wrong.

A demonstration of caring is vitally important to the establishment of rapport. If the negotiator does not even bother to get the subject's name right, it will be difficult to convince him that the negotiator cares about him in any other way.

Early on, do not forget to ask the subject to come out. Sometimes subjects do not come out because a negotiator, officer, or deputy did not think to ask. A state investigator/negotiator arrived on the scene of a barricade a few hours into the incident. Being the only trained negotiator on scene, he made contact with the subject, introduced himself and said, "I want you to put your weapon down and come out the front door with your hands where we can see them."

The subject responded with, "Okay. I'm coming out."

The negotiator, not expecting the subject to immediately surrender and thinking that perhaps he had misunderstood, again said, "Now, I want you to put the weapon down and come out the front door with your hands where we can see them."

The subject repeated, "Okay. I'm coming out."

The negotiator being unable to resist said, "Okay. Good, but why?"

The subject said, "The deputies told me if I came out of the house with my rifle there was going to be trouble so I just stayed inside. I'm coming out."

Often, officers or deputies not trained in crisis negotiation are first on the scene. Commonly, they have made contact with the subject and have opened a dialogue. If they are doing well in terms of rapport-building and calming the subject, leave them in place and have a trained negotiator coach them through the ordeal. Leaving the officers in place if they are reasonably comfortable with the job and are doing well is a good idea for several reasons.

Morale is one good reason. Officers or deputies often feel that this incident is their call and the "big boys" are now coming in to take it away from them. As a practical matter, it is a good idea to keep them on scene because they were the first there. Invariably, as soon as they drive off, investigators realize that some important question was not asked. Now, the officer or deputy is on the other side of the county, off duty, or cannot be located.

If the officer is doing a good job, sometimes the subject does not want to change negotiators. On one occasion, a tactical officer made first contact with the subject and, though being uncomfortable in the role of negotiator, opened a dialogue with him. The tactical officer told the bad guy that a particular negotiator would be arriving soon and that the negotiator was a good guy who could get things done. When the negotiator did arrive and attempted to take over the negotiation, the subject said, "I don't want to talk to you. I want to talk to the other guy."

Some subjects will invest a lot in the first officer they talk to. They seem to be reassured by the presence of the police, and especially by the first officer to make contact.

Common Means of Communication

Often law enforcement officers will begin communicating with the subject via bullhorn. A bullhorn gets his attention and he can be given instructions while still refusing to answer the telephone. The problem with a bullhorn is its lack of privacy and intimacy. Negotiators talk to people about very private, intimate, personal problems and feelings as they attempt to build a rapport with the subject. Few subjects will be amenable to discussing their personal problems by shouting them to the negotiator.

When communicating with the subject by direct voice, over a bullhorn or speakers, negotiators should remember to do so from cover, that is, from behind something that will stop a bullet. Subjects have been known to shoot at the sound of the negotiator's voice. If placing speakers around an objective, do not call out over the speakers until the person placing the speakers is well out of the way.

Exposed face-to-face should be avoided if at all possible and will be discussed later in this chapter. Direct voice from a position cover (not concealment) is better, but the telephone is generally considered the best form of communication for a variety of reasons.

Telephones allow negotiators to more readily confer with their backup regarding developing information and negotiation tactics. Telephones, too, are obviously safer. It is also easier to hang up than to stop a face-to-face conversation. Commercially built crisis telephones are especially good because of their wide variety of features, including tape-recording capability, multiple headsets, and other options. It is imperative that negotiators maintain familiarity with any specialized equipment. In the middle of the night with shots being fired is not the time to be trying to figure out how a piece of communications equipment works.

Modern telephone systems have changed negotiation techniques and concerns over the last 20 years. At one time, there was often no more than one telephone in a house. If the subject repeatedly picked up the telephone on the first ring and the only telephone was in the kitchen, the negotiators could tell the tactical team where the subject was with some degree of confidence. No longer is that true. The advent of cordless and wireless telephones and specialized telephone features has changed the scene considerably.

A negotiator tells the story of working a situation for several hours before the subject said he would come out, but nothing happened. The negotiator called the subject one more time. The subject provided an address on the other side of the city, 20 minutes away. The subject's telephone was on call forwarding.

The ideal negotiation site is one with little background noise to be heard by the subject and act as a distraction to the negotiator. It should have sufficient telephones for negotiators to maintain contact with the subject, command, investigators, tactical personnel, and others. Obviously, it should be out of the subject's line of fire.

The Role of Time

The importance of the passage of time, especially in spontaneous sieges, is difficult to overstate. Persons who are in a crisis state will change in a relatively short period of time, that is, a few hours. With the passage of time and the venting of emotion, the subject will begin to calm down and become more rational.

Over time, basic human needs increase. The subject will become hungry, thirsty, and tired, get hot or cold, need a toilet, cigarette, drink, or drug. It is when he begins to realize that he must go through the negotiator to get his needs met that the power gradually shifts in the negotiator's favor.

Hostages may find opportunities to escape as time passes, but negotiators should not count on hostages or victims escaping even if given what appears to be a clear opportunity to do so. Negotiators should keep in mind that hostages have probably been threatened and feel as if they are betting their lives that their escape attempt will be successful. They may also feel that if their escape is successful, the subject will harm the remaining hostages.

Good decision making does not just happen. Good decision making requires accurate information and the gathering of such information takes time. Satisfactory decisions are based on good information, training, experience, and attitude. Sometimes bad decisions are made in spite of good information. No negotiator should assume that good information will somehow automatically result in good decisions.

No one wants to make a deal with someone they do not trust. It is essential that the negotiator establish a condition of trust and rapport with the subject over time.

Stalling Techniques

To obtain the beneficial effects of the passage of time it is often necessary for the negotiator to stall. The negotiator's primary stalling tactic should be the employment of active-listening skills, not telling lies. Active-listening skills, as mentioned earlier, help the negotiator calm the subject, establish rapport, gather information, and gain time. The benefits of active listening far exceed the pitfalls of lying and the possibility of being caught in such lies.

No one is suggesting that the negotiator should never lie if it suits a particular purpose and there is no readily apparent way around the lie. Stalling, itself, is a lie. Lying, especially in situations requiring shift changes, is extremely hazardous in terms of negotiator credibility. The bottom line for negotiators is that they should avoid lying but, if they must, do not get caught at it.

Concerns that Arise with the Passage of Time

There is a down side to the passage of time and, beyond some point, the advantages of stalling for time will diminish. A major problem is exhaustion on the part of the subject, negotiators, tactical personnel, and commanders. All crisis team members must be relieved on a timely basis. Though 12 hours is probably too long to be actively negotiating, most teams establish 12-hour shifts.

Typically, however, the first shift in long sieges will be extraordinarily long. Apparently, personnel believe the incident will end soon, want to be on scene for the resolution, and feel that if they leave they will miss the action.

It often becomes difficult to get personnel to leave for rest or even run errands. No one wants to go home and have his son to expectantly ask, "Hey, Dad, when that bad guy was shot today, what did you do?" and have to answer, "Well son, I was down at McDonald's buying burgers for the team and I missed the whole thing."

Exhaustion can lead to thinking that is fuzzy at best and, at worst, irrational. For example, what sounds like a good idea at 3:00 a.m. after 18 hours of high stress may not sound quite so good in the morning or later in court.

Profound exhaustion can even lead to transient psychotic breaks. Many officers have reported working a midnight shift and standing on the brakes of their patrol cars erroneously believing something has darted out in front of them. Their response to something they thought they saw was the result of exhaustion.

Negotiators want to wear the subject down but only to a certain point. Any further exhaustion is not the optimal state of mind, especially for a hostage taker or a drunken, abusive husband with a gun to his wife's head.

Boredom is another problem that sometimes leads to carelessness and even unprofessional behavior. Law enforcement officers do not join the profession because they enjoy a quiet lifestyle. Many become officers and deputies because, among other reasons, they enjoy the action and excitement. It is difficult for most people to just wait hour after hour or day after day but, for action-oriented people, this waiting is even more difficult.

The creeping-up effect occurs in three different varieties. Negotiators who were initially safely behind a position of cover are seen to be standing in a doorway, for example. This occurrence is so frequent some experienced teams will have the secondary negotiator hold onto the primary's belt so he or she does not step out into the subject's line of fire. If appropriate to the circumstances, it might not be a bad idea for negotiators to actually draw a chalk line on the floor. The chalk line indicates to the negotiator, "Step over this line and you will be in the line of fire."

A problem on the inner perimeter is that people who have no business to be there start gathering. Officers want to be close to the action. On the outer perimeter, officers, again, start moving in closer and, coupled with becoming bored with manning the outer perimeter, become careless.

Injuries, illness, and other medical problems are always a concern as an incident advances through the hours. The concern is that the medical situation might be deteriorating as time passes.

The pressure for resolution is sometimes called the "action imperative." Pressure for resolution can come from commanders who are concerned about a variety of issues including the cost of overtime, inconvenience to the city, manpower, the appearance of not being tough, frustration, etc. Negotiators and tactical personnel can also be pushed to "do something, anything." Never, ever, take an action just to be "doing something."

In the U. S., the vast majority of law enforcement agencies have fewer than 10 officers or deputies, so manpower and money in these smaller agencies is always a problem. There are not enough people to properly man an incident if left to their own resources. In several states, it is not uncommon for a law enforcement agency to have two people, the chief and his wife, who is the dispatcher.

Yet, in major cities, using 50 to 60 people to work a barricade would not be unusual.

Even in larger cities where manpower may be plentiful, there could be a problem in finding sufficient specialized personnel such as sniper/observers, negotiators, and tactical personnel for more than one shift. Contingency plans should be in place for multiple shifts of manpower with the necessary special skills.

In several areas around the country, law enforcement agencies have put together countywide tactical and negotiation teams. Each agency signatory to the agreement provides money and manpower. In the event of a major incident, each agency provides a limited number of people. In this way, no single incident is going to wipe out an overtime budget and the manpower concerns are minimized. As one chief lamented, "If I use eight people to work a barricade situation tonight, who will I put on the street tomorrow?"

The effects of drugs, alcohol, and withdrawal over time are a common concern. Some law enforcement agencies have estimated as few as 40 percent of their involvement in negotiated incidents include drugs or alcohol. More agencies, though, have said that all of their incidents have involved drugs and/or alcohol. Some negotiators claim that everyone that they negotiate with is under the influence of something. The complex question then is, as this incident proceeds, will the potential for violence increase or recede? Is the subject going to be more dangerous under the influence or in withdrawal? A medical opinion during an incident might not be a bad idea.

Prolonged incidents very commonly cause inconvenience to a city and neighborhoods. People may need to be evacuated from their homes or traffic flow may be disrupted. In one case, a fugitive was observed driving away from a residence. Federal agents gave chase. The subject stopped his vehicle on an on-ramp to an interstate highway on a Friday afternoon in a major city, causing the city to fill with irate commuters. He threatened to kill his dog and himself before finally surrendering at 9:30 p.m. Throughout the ordeal, the federal agents and state police were receiving telephone calls from the mayor's office demanding that something, anything be done.

Media and public attention can be a major problem over time. Crowds of media personnel and the public can get in the way of law enforcement and other emergency vehicles.

Deadlines

The guidelines concerning deadlines that negotiators have been using since the 1970s have changed very little. Upon receipt of a deadline, log it and inform command. It is still recommended that negotiators contact the subject before the deadline and engage the subject in conversation as the deadline expires. Even if the subject is aware that the deadline is passing, the negotiator, by talking to him, gives him a graceful way out of his threatened violence. The negotiator should avoid referring to the subject's deadline when talking to him. Both parties know the deadline is expiring and its expiration goes unmentioned.

Negotiators should not set a deadline on themselves by promising anything at a specified time. For example, a negotiator should not promise the delivery of coffee within 10 minutes. When the coffee is not delivered at the specified time, subjects get very angry. They are certain the negotiator lied and is deliberately giving them the run around.

Use the excuse of turmoil and confusion, if necessary, for not meeting deadlines. In general, negotiators should attempt to take the credit for anything good that happens and blame others for any problems and misunderstandings.

Demands

In general, the idea of a negotiator's never saying "no" to a demand is still a good one. But keep in mind that not saying "no" is not the same as saying "yes." Negotiators ought to remain open-minded and flexible in dealing with demands—even those they know will not be met. Sometimes, though, the subject knows that his demands will not be met. In these circumstances, the harsh, unvarnished truth will gain the negotiator credibility.

Negotiators should always have the other side make the first offer in terms of how many hostages are released. It would be a serious error for negotiators to ask for one hostage, for example, when the subject would have been willing to release two. It is difficult for the negotiator to determine the worth of the hostages to the subject so let him make the first offer. Remember that command must authorize all agreements.

An idea that some negotiators seem to have gotten away from is to get something in return for everything the negotiator gives the subject. Some negotiators seem to feel that giving the subject small things such as a cigarette will help in the rapport-building process. Other negotiators believe that merely giving the subject something achieves nothing and may even be detrimental to the negotiating process. Most of the people with whom negotiators work will view the yielding to requests and demands as a sign of weakness and not feel at all indebted or appreciative toward the negotiator.

The act of giving in to the subject also perpetuates the idea that he is in control. It is recommended here that the negotiator establish a quid pro quo and get something in return for everything given to the subject even if it is only a promise of change in behavior.

Along the same line of thought, the negotiator should make the subject work for everything he receives from the authorities. Nothing should be easy for him. Negotiators should portray themselves as well meaning but bumbling, strong but approachable and empathetic. Giving in to the subject works against that image. It follows then that the negotiator should not raise the subject's aspirations or expectations by giving him too much too soon.

Do not request demands either. Asking for demands may initiate or perpetuate feelings of power. Negotiators want to gradually move the subject away from the idea that his demands will be met. Do not ask for trouble.

The presentation of demands can be a major development in the evolution of a crisis. As with all major developments, log the demands and inform command. It is important to log demands so that negotiators can accurately testify at a later date should their testimony be required. Negotiators tend to think that they will never forget how a particular incident unfolded but due to stress they do forget. At the same time, and for some of the same reasons, negotiators should log everything they give the subject and remind him what they have given him, if necessary.

Never dismiss a demand as being inconsequential. If the demand is important to the subject, it is important to the negotiator. In fact, if a demand seems inconsequential or even inappropriate to the negotiator, it might be a topic to follow up on. The negotiator could be missing something.

Do not bring up demands that he has not mentioned for awhile unless it is to your advantage. In fact, it may not be a good idea to initiate any dialogue on demands. Let him bring up the topic each time.

Be prepared for, but be very careful about, suggesting alternatives during a siege. If the subject is displaying any signs of paranoia, the suggestion of alternatives may evoke a reaction. Or, if the negotiator's well-intended suggestion does not work out, the negotiator should be ready to take the brunt of the subject's frustration. Typically, subjects imbue negotiators with more power than they actually have. Anything that goes wrong with the negotiator's suggestion will come back to haunt the negotiator and the subject may even believe that the negotiator set him up for failure.

Subject's Needs

As an incident progresses, the negotiator becomes the only person through whom the subject's needs are met. Part of a negotiator's task is to identify the subject's needs and use them to obtain resolution of the incident. Sometimes negotiators will hear mental health professionals talking about instrumental and expressive needs. Instrumental needs are the spoken needs and include such things as food, water, getaway car, money, cigarettes, beer, and comfort items.

Expressive needs are often unspoken and include acceptance, belonging, affection, power, and self-worth. It is important to listen for expressive needs that are not being met. Some situations are based entirely on expressive needs. Occasionally, negotiators may wonder among themselves what it will take to end an incident when the negotiation is otherwise going well but the subject just will not surrender. At this point, the negotiation team should be thinking about expressive needs and what the subject wants out of the incident that he has not mentioned.

One hostage taker took hostages on three occasions. The first two incidents took place at the same location where it seemed that the subject had no previous connection whatsoever. The likeliest explanation for his choice of this location was that it is was across the street from a television station. His demands were similar in all three incidents in that he wanted to talk to a number of old friends, family members, and others. These individuals were permitted to speak to him and all said basically the same thing, "Why are you doing this? You know we love you. Please don't do this. Don't hurt those people. Don't hurt yourself." After getting his fill of attention, he surrendered.

During the third incident at a different location, the whole scenario began once more. He demanded to speak to friends and relatives; they were again permitted to speak and they again professed their love for him and implored him not to hurt himself or anyone else. After long hours of the same, a negotiator got on the telephone and said, "Okay, that's it. From now on you speak to no one but me, no one."

The subject cried, "You're going to kill me, aren't you? Aren't you?"

The negotiator, after a pause that was apparently a bit too long for the subject, attempted to reassure him by saying, "No. We're not going to kill you."

Now, in the subject's mind, the incident was getting serious. He surrendered a short time later. No one repeats an act unless they are getting something they want out of it. In these incidents, the subject was getting what he wanted, attention. The only time people paid any attention to him was when he took hostages, so he did it three times. After the third occasion, he finally received a lengthy prison term.

The subject's shift from instrumental needs to expressive needs may indicate that he is developing some trust in the negotiator and rapport is being established. It is relatively easy to talk about one's instrumental needs. For example, "I'm thirsty. Send me a beer in here."

On the other hand, it is much more difficult for a subject to talk about his expressive needs such as "I'm no good. I've never been able to hold a job. I've never been able to keep a woman. No wonder she left me."

It would appear that a negotiator is making progress in establishing rapport if the subject is talking about expressive needs because they tend to be much more personal. Expressive needs are a topic of conversation only with someone a person trusts.

Another way to address expressive needs is to talk to the subject about a topic he feels good about. A negotiator who was working with a hostage taker whose usual occupation was truck salesman said, "While we are working on your demands there is something I would like to ask."

The subject said, "What's that?"

"I am in the market for a pickup truck and I'm not sure what kind to buy. What do you suggest?"

The subject said, "Well, what are you going to use it for?" The subject and negotiator then talked for more than an hour about the pros and cons of the various brands.

Finally, the negotiator said, "Maybe we should get back to business here."

To which the subject replied, "Hey, I'm just going to throw it in. I know you guys are not going to give me what I want. If you want to know anything else about trucks, you'll know where to find me."

Another negotiator arrested a carpenter and was interviewing the man at his desk. The officer had taken a large hunting knife from the subject and placed it in his desk drawer but neglected to close the drawer. The subject reached into the drawer, retrieved the knife then held it to his abdomen while proclaiming his suicidal intent. The officer saw the end of his career staring him in the face with a prisoner in his custody committing suicide.

After some dialogue, the officer said, "I understand you're a carpenter. I'm trying to build a garden shed behind my house but I can't even drive a nail straight. I could go to school for years and never be able to do what you do. Where'd you learn to do that?"

The subject then went on to tell the negotiator how he had learned his carpentry skills. After some time had passed, the subject put the knife down, surrendered, and said, "When I get out, I'd be glad to help you with that garden shed."

Asking the subject's advice about a topic where he feels competent is very similar to the "hook" described in the chapter on suicide. This topic is an area where he feels good about himself. The negotiator is an authority figure asking his advice and that also builds up his self esteem. The topic is away from the subject's concerns that are driving the incident. It is a very effective technique that allows the subject to calm down, it passes time, and builds the subject's self esteem all at the same time.

Actually, talking to the subject in a conversational manner often leads to unexpected resolutions. Another negotiator was working with a barricaded subject. The negotiation seemed to be going well but the subject, who was not in a position to hurt anyone, refused to come out. The negotiator, becoming increasingly frustrated, said,

"I'm going home for some red beans, rice, and ham and I'll be back in an hour or so."

The subject named a small town back in the hills and asked if the negotiator was familiar with it. The negotiator said that he was and offered that he was from a neighboring town back in the hills. The subject then said, "Reckon if I come out I can get some red beans, rice, and ham?"

The negotiator said, "I think we can do that."

The subject said, "Good, I'm coming out."

Sometimes, it is very difficult to predict what technique might be effective for a negotiator. By merely talking to the subject, negotiators sometimes hit on topics that lead to a resolution.

Communication Recommendations

Some standard communication recommendations include the following:

- Be supportive as long as the subject is rational.
- If you are not sure what the subject meant, ask.
- Downplay what the subject has done so far.
- Avoid using profanity.
- Be yourself.
- Choose your words, tone, and manner very carefully.
- Adapt your conversation to his educational and vocabulary level.
- Speak slowly and calmly.
- Avoid saying "no" but lower expectations by creating doubt that the demands will be fulfilled.
- When talking to the subject avoid being distracted.
- Minimize and be aware of your background noises.
- Strive for honesty to ensure credibility.

Double Check All Intelligence

Double checking all information will save money, embarrassment, and lives. A patrol officer reported standing at the front door of a residence with his weapon drawn and pointed at a subject who was in a rage and brandishing a large hunting knife. A woman on the front lawn was screaming and calling out, "My baby! My baby!"

Several times the subject approached a bundle on a couch that the officer took to be the baby. Each time the officer came close to firing to protect the baby. At the conclusion of the incident, the "baby" proved to be a 17-year-old girl who was hiding in a back closet and the bundle thought to be the baby was a rolled-up blanket. The officer, who was clearly shaken by the incident, said, "I nearly killed the guy for approaching a rolled-up blanket."

On another occasion, a negotiator made contact with an estranged husband who had kidnapped his children. The tactical team responded to an address provided by the subject's wife. The negotiator opened a dialogue and the subject appeared to be amenable to the negotiator's suggestions. He told the negotiator, "Hang on. I want to get on the downstairs phone. I'm afraid that I will wake up the kids talking on this one."

The negotiator turned to a tactical representative and said, "He's going downstairs."

The tactical team member said, "The house we have surrounded has no downstairs."

The negotiator reinterviewed the mother, who was in a nearby room. She said, "Well, it is either 123 Elm Street or 223 Elm Street." The subject was finally located at 223 Elm Street.

Another negotiator reported that he had been on the telephone for many hours when the subject finally said, "Okay. I'm coming out."

A few minutes passed and nothing happened. The subject then got back on the telephone. The negotiator said, "I thought you told me that you were coming out."

The subject responded with, "I tried to but a cop on the front porch pushed me back into the house and said there was a barricade situation next door and that I should stay inside."

Still another negotiator said he, too, had been negotiating for several hours. The subject agreed to give up but then nothing happened until they saw the subject three houses down the block calling out, "Hey, over here."

Non-Response Situations

Inadequately checked intelligence is but one reason for non-response situations. More than one law enforcement agency has negotiated for hours with an empty house. Perhaps the subject was never there or maybe he escaped. He may not be responding for any number of reasons. Never assume, though, that he is gone or dead.

Consider the following:

- The subject cannot hear the negotiator for some reason, such as his location in the house or the mere distance from negotiator to subject. Or, the subject may be deaf. Negotiators have worked with deaf-mute people on several occasions.
- The negotiator cannot hear the subject. There have been occasions where the subject was responding but the negotiator could not hear him and the negotiator thought he was in a non-response situation.
- The subject cannot understand the negotiator. Language differences have been and will continue to be, a problem.
- The subject is sleeping, passed out, unconscious, or dead. The subject may have passed out from the use of drugs or alcohol. Or, perhaps he is unconscious or dead from illness, injuries, or wounds.
- Some subjects apparently hope to avoid detection, arrest, and incarceration by not responding to the negotiator. Their hope is that if they do not respond to the negotiator, the police will go away and they will not have to go to jail.
- Subjects fear making themselves mentally and physically vulnerable. Some subjects clearly feel that if they respond, the negotiator will hear the fear in their voices and that will make them more vulnerable. Others fear the tactical team will shoot at the sound of their voices.
- Some subjects believe they have done nothing wrong. Primarily, in domestic situations, the abusive husband or boyfriend will not respond because, to their way of thinking they have done nothing wrong, the police have no business being there, so they just do not answer.
- Some suicidal persons will not respond because they lack the energy to do so. Others may be setting a trap. A negotiator recalled an incident where the subject was talking suicide for several hours when a shot rang out. After repeated unsuccessful attempts to re-contact the subject and believing that the subject had killed himself, the tactical team made

entry. The subject had fortified himself, and as the first tactical member crossed the threshold he was hit in the chest with a shotgun blast that blew him off the front porch. Fortunately, the officer was wearing body armor and survived.

Never assume the subject has committed suicide because a shot was fired. If an entry is made, assume that he is alive and waiting for the entry team.

Negotiators should continue to elicit a response from the subject via reassuring and nonthreatening statements over a bullhorn or speakers. He or she may attempt to work up to a dialogue by suggesting nonverbal methods of response to the subject by saying, for example, "If you can hear me, flick the lights on and off."

Hostage Injuries

The two most critical times for the safety of the hostages are generally believed to be at the initial confrontation and during a police entry to rescue them.

In an aircraft hijacking research project conducted by the FBI and the University of Louisville School of Medicine, Department of Psychiatry, hijackings were divided into complete and incomplete hijackings. Completed hijackings were those where the hijacker arrived at his demanded destination. Incomplete hijackings were those where he did not. Interestingly enough, in the hijackings originating on U.S. soil, there was not a single death or injury during the completed hijackings.

The Stockholm Syndrome

The Stockholm Syndrome takes it name from an August, 1973 bank robbery in Stockholm, Sweden. Two subjects, for a total of 131 hours, held four bank employees. During this incident the hostages and subjects developed a strong bond that sparked the interest of the authorities and mental health professionals alike.

The Stockholm Syndrome consists of one or more of the following:

- The hostages will begin to have positive feelings toward their captors. Hostages will begin to say things like, "He's not such a bad guy. He doesn't want to hurt us."
- The hostages will begin to have negative feelings toward the authorities. The hostages might add, "He'll only hurt us because you are being unreasonable and are pushing him into it."
- The subject will begin to develop positive feelings toward his hostages.

It is this third factor that the authorities attempt to promote to save lives in hostage situations.

Some observers erroneously refer to the relationship developed between the subject and negotiator as the Stockholm Syndrome. It is believed that this relationship is based on a totally different psychological dynamic from that relationship developed between hostage taker and hostages.

Negotiators should not expect to see the Stockholm syndrome if the victim and the subject have had a previous relationship. One would not expect to see its development in domestic situations, for example.

There are a number of factors that affect the development of the Stockholm Syndrome. Obviously, at least some time must pass. Some observers believe it can occur in as little as 10 minutes.

In the study of aircraft hijackings referred to above, it was determined that the Stockholm Syndrome must be initiated by the subject. If the once-frightening subject does something positive for his victims, they are more likely to respond with sympathetic feelings toward him.

The nature of the contact between the subject and hostages appears to be among the decisive factors. A description of those contacts is listed below:

- Positive contact: If the subject initiates positive contact between himself and the hostages, the Stockholm Syndrome is most probable. Positive contact means that he does something that the hostages feel good about. For example, he might tell the hostages not to worry about anything they may hear him tell the police and that he really means them no harm. He might say that he has to talk to the police like that

and threaten to do the hostages harm or the police will come in and kill all of them.
- Negative contact: If the subject abuses the hostages, there will be no Stockholm Syndrome.
- Positive contact followed by negative contact: The Stockholm Syndrome initiated by early positive contact can be overcome by the subject's later abusive behavior.
- Negative contact followed by positive contact: Sometimes, the subject will initially abuse the hostages and later apologize for his behavior. He justifies his behavior to the hostages by telling them he was afraid of them or the police. This scenario may result in the development of the Stockholm Syndrome.
- No contact between subject and hostages: If there is no contact between the subject and hostages, no relationship will develop. In most aircraft hijackings, for example, the subject is often up front with the crew and has little or no contact with the passengers.

Negotiators' Relationship to the Hostages and Victims

Negotiators should not indicate that they are more concerned about the victim's welfare than the subject's. They should indicate that they want to help resolve the subject's problem, particularly in spontaneous sieges where the subject is in emotional turmoil and much of that emotion, especially anger, is being directed at his victim.

Negotiators are rightly concerned about the victim but it is the subject's emotional reaction to his circumstances and his subsequent behavior that make the situation into a crisis for the authorities. Spending a lot of time talking about or with the victims does not resolve his problem and satisfactorily resolving his problem is what concludes the incident. Be aware though, that the victims and hostages will not like the fact that the negotiator is talking about the subject's problems, bargaining for their lives and is not paying much attention to them.

Getting to know the hostages and victims may well put the negotiator under additional stress. Negotiating for the lives of strangers is difficult enough. Negotiating for the lives of people who are now known to the negotiator is even more difficult.

Keep the Stockholm Syndrome in mind when talking to the hostages. Negotiators should be very careful about confiding in the hostages because they may not be totally aligned with the negotiator's view of the incident. The hostages' ambivalent feelings mean that the authorities should be wary of any intelligence provided by them.

Medical Problems in High-Stress Situations

Early in an incident, it is a good idea to ask, "Is there anyone in there with any medical problems I ought to know about?"

By asking the question in just this way, the negotiator is asking about everyone—the subject as well as hostages or victims. Inquiring about any medical problems leaves the question wide open, from injuries and illness to headaches and chest pains. The "I ought to know about" part of the sentence indicates the negotiator's personal concern about everyone.

When the incident settles down somewhat, double check. Ask the subject if he is all right and have him ask each victim or hostage about any immediate or continuing medical problems they may have. The concern here is that the subject or any of the individuals with him may need medication for any one of many conditions as time passes. By asking the victims about their medical condition, the subject will get to know the victims as people and thereby promote the Stockholm syndrome.

High stress can lead to a wide variety of large and small medical conditions in both the short and long run (see Table 6.1). In addition to the medical ailments encountered when gathering a group of people at random, as they are in a hostage situation, the addition of high stress results in more problems.

Common Subject Weaknesses

Even in deliberate sieges where there is at least a modicum of planning, hostage takers do not anticipate sick or injured hostages or the fact that people may require medication. Negotiators should try to get the sick, injured, wounded, or persons needing medication out first. Not only for the obvious medical reasons but because

Table 6.1 Potential Medical Problems in High-Stress Incidents

Physical Changes	Disorders
Cardiovascular system	Chest pains, heart attacks
Respiratory system	Hyperventilation, asthma attacks
Gastrointestinal/urinary changes	Loss of control
Tension	Chest pain, back pain, headaches
Adrenaline	Diabetes, shakes, tremors, increased alertness, insomnia, restlessness
Digestive system	Acid stomach and stomach pain

they are the easiest to be released. The subject does not want them in there because they are unsettling everyone. Getting the sick and injured out also establishes a good precedent for the negotiator and subject working together and sets the stage for additional hostage releases.

Another common weakness is that subjects tend to let their guard down when they believe they have finally won. A bank robber holding a hostage demanded a getaway car on his deadline. His mental-health professional, who was on scene, believed he would kill his hostage with or without the car. After many hours, the negotiator finally said, "Okay. You win. The car is out front. Make sure it is where you want it."

For the first time all day, the subject went to the front of the bank, looked out the glass door and was shot through the heart by a sniper located across the street. The subject had thought he had won and he let his guard down.

Negotiators have been known to let their guard down, too. When they think they have finally won, they start to get careless. This turn of events is particularly dangerous if the subject insists on surrendering to the negotiator and no one else. Surrendering to the tactical team is the preferred mode of surrender, but if the subject is surrendering to the negotiator, the surrender should be carefully choreographed with the tactical team including sniper or observer teams. A situation is never over for a negotiator until the subject is in handcuffs and being led away.

Telephone Negotiation Techniques

Telephone negotiations are the safest for negotiators and with some planning and preparation can be the most effective form of negotiation. The first order of business is to find a location where the negotiator can concentrate and avoid distraction. Before calling, negotiators should write down a list of ideas they want to mention. They should rehearse what they will say and how it will be said with their secondary negotiators. Part of the preparation process is to anticipate the subject's tactics and have all relevant intelligence at hand. Finally, it helps to be the one who initiates the call, because the caller has had time to prepare. And, at all times, negotiators must remember to use active listening techniques.

Taping the Negotiation

First, be aware of state laws that govern the taping of telephone conversations. During a negotiation team training session, invite a legal adviser in to discuss issues such as negotiator liability issues, taping the negotiation, listening devices, search and seizure, and all of the other legal questions that go along with a negotiation effort.

Tape recording the conversation with the subject can be a great aid to the negotiation process. In the heat of "battle," important bits of information and themes can be overlooked. Reviewing the last dialogue with the subject can help bring these items to light.

The taped negotiations provide very dramatic evidence of the subject's mental state contemporaneous with the crime. During mental-health examinations and court hearings some time later, when he has had an opportunity to calm down, think things over, had the advice of counsel, and has something to gain by playing a role, he may seem like a totally different person from the one the negotiator encountered during the standoff.

The tapes are also dramatic evidence of the subject's actions, including his behavior and threats against the hostages and victims. During one incident in which two people, a woman and a baby, died, the negotiation was tape-recorded. When the tapes were played in court, the jurors, subject, and judge could all hear the baby crying for its mother in the background. Virtually all listeners in the courtroom were wiping tears from their cheeks. The subject was sentenced to 40 years without parole.

A negotiation does not require Miranda warnings because the subject is not in custody or being interrogated. If, during the negotiation, the subject admits to crimes previous to the siege, those admissions on tape are good evidence of those crimes. A word of caution to negotiators, do not turn your negotiation into an interrogation. The court decisions with respect to the Miranda warnings have been close thus far in the favor of law enforcement.

Some negotiators are still concerned over the possibility that they will be sued and the tape-recorded negotiation will be evidence against them. Living with the threat of lawsuits is part of being in law enforcement. People can sue over anything an officer does. Historically, taped negotiations have done far more good than harm in the defense of negotiators and their agencies. As long as negotiators adhere to the guidelines of their training, it will be difficult to successfully sue them. To call forth a valid lawsuit, negotiators must do something way out of line with their training. Rather than being incriminating, the tapes will provide evidence of the fact that negotiators did everything they could—and should—have done.

The taped negotiations are good for research, that is, the negotiator's personal research on issues and more-formal academic research that may advance knowledge of negotiation. For training purposes, it is useful to review with team members the last negotiated incident. In the classroom, the tapes can be difficult to use unless they are unusually good in quality or sensational.

Exposed Face-to-Face Considerations

Negotiator should strive to avoid face-to-face contact with the subject especially if a firearm is involved. Sometimes, however, officers and deputies, as a result of unforeseen circumstances, find themselves unable to avoid a face-to-face situation. If the subject does have a firearm, the prudent action would be to back off and reopen negotiations from a position of cover. If the subject is armed with something other than a firearm it may still be judicious to find a safer location for the reasons discussed earlier.

While in no way advocating face-to-face negotiations, if the negotiator or officer is considering such a confrontation, as with a suicidal jumper, negotiators should think about the following:

- Consider the advantages vs. the risks of being face-to-face.
- Obtain a promise of negotiator safety from the subject.
- Never knowingly walk into a situation where a firearm might be pointed at them.
- For negotiators to turn their backs depersonalizes them. It is not advisable to leave suicidal persons alone. If negotiators must leave, they should obtain a promise that no suicidal action will take place in their absence, give a promise to return soon, then back away from the subject.
- Always leave an escape route. Negotiators should ensure that they can readily move to a safer position.
- Never work with more than one subject at a time. No one can watch two people at the same time.
- Be aware of body space. Paranoid and frightened persons will require a great deal of body space. If a negotiator is advancing toward the subject and he starts to back up, the negotiator should stop advancing and take a step back.
- Maintain adequate cover. Make sure the negotiator's position is cover and not merely concealment. A rock wall is cover. An azalea bush is concealment. If the negotiator does not have adequate cover, find some or make the current position into cover by putting bulletproof materials between the negotiator and subject. Kevlar blankets or body armor can be hung from a wall or the negotiator can use a ballistic shield.
- Assess your own anxiety. If negotiators are not comfortable in terms of their anxiety it is going to be difficult to convince the subject there is nothing to worry about. Experienced negotiators or officers should never ignore their gut feeling about an incident.
- Wear body armor.
- Always carry a weapon. The idea that negotiators should be unarmed is an old concept. Negotiators should be armed

with the weapon they feel most comfortable carrying and are authorized to carry.
- Coordinate tactical back up. Any time the negotiator is on the inner perimeter, all movements must be coordinated with the tactical component.
- Never enter the subject's space when there is an indication of explosives being present. Respect the possibility that any bomb threat could be real.

Manipulation of Anxiety

Deliberately manipulating the subject's anxiety level is an outmoded technique that many departments have abandoned as being too dangerous. Subjects are generally very fearful, and any law enforcement action that could even be perceived as aggressive should be carried out very carefully or avoided altogether, as it could evoke a violent response from the subject.

Potential Problem Words and Phrases

Be alert for any words or phrases that draw an emotional response. If the reason for the response is not clear, the basis for this reaction should be determined through the negotiation process and investigation. No list of potential problem words or phrases will ever be complete because people and their circumstances are unique. Negotiators should put their energy into listening rather than trying to remember a list of words to be avoided.

A negotiator inadvertently declared to a suicidal individual in a parked car, "I think that's our best shot." The negotiator, immediately realizing what he had said, winced.

The subject laughed and said, "I don't guess you should have said that."

Negotiation errors are much easier to overcome than tactical errors, and that is the beauty and power of negotiation. If a particular technique is not working, the negotiator should move on and try something else.

Indicators of Negotiation Progress

People communicate on two levels—the content, or factual, level and the emotional level. In measuring negotiation progress, negotiators continue to look at the same two levels. During the progress of the negotiation, the content of the subject's communications will shift from threatening, violent language to nonthreatening, nonviolent language. There will also be a readiness, even eagerness, to disclose personal information. The content of his remarks will shift from emotional to rational content. The negotiator will observe a willingness to discuss topics unrelated to the incident as the subject settles down emotionally and engages the negotiator in what sounds more like a conversation than negotiation.

In addition to content and emotion, the form of the subject's communications will change with progress. The subject's voice level will be much more normal, that is, he will not be screaming. His speech will be at a much less rapid rate. Early on in the negotiation, often he might have been yelling and talking rapidly. Now, with progress, he is conversing in conversational tones at a normal rate of speech. Negotiators will notice that conversations will be of increased length.

In one hostage-taking incident, the subject said virtually nothing for 31 hours. Before the incident was over, he wanted to stay on the telephone with the negotiator and not be left alone. This increased willingness or desire to speak with the authorities may also be indicated by the number of times the subject initiates a conversation with the negotiator.

One negotiator counted the number of obscenities and vulgarities spoken by the subject in 15-minute increments. Over time, as the subject calmed down and rapport was established, the subject used fewer and fewer expletives.

Some negotiators view other developments as indicators of progress. Any reduction in violent behavior such as the subject's randomly firing his weapon can be viewed as negotiation progress. The release of hostages, and deadlines passing without incident are also hopeful indicators. Certainly, the establishment of a rapport between the negotiator and the hostage taker is a good sign, as is increased willingness to follow the negotiator's suggestions.

Potential Problem Areas with the Media

The media can cause crisis-management personnel problems of all kinds. In fact, it might not be a bad idea to liven up negotiator training sessions by inviting local reporters to discuss issues of mutual interest, or invite them to an exercise.

During an incident, reporters should be briefed as to what has transpired. No reporters will go back to their bosses and report that the law enforcement personnel would not talk to them so they have no story. If law enforcement representatives do not talk to them, the media will air interviews with witnesses, families of the subject and the victims, politicians, government officials, and released hostages. Reporters, broadcast and print, will go back to the office with a story gleaned from any and all sources who might have a sound byte to add to the situation. They might as well have law enforcement's version of the incident.

During a prison hostage situation, the media went on the air with, "It looks like this incident is about to come to a tactical resolution. Additional tactical personnel are arriving on scene and we'll be here at the prison to cover this development."

Meanwhile, the inmates, who were watching television, were going berserk. Negotiators immediately contacted them and said, "You know our shift-change schedule. Look at the time. You know we haven't lied to you. It's only a shift change." The inmate replied, "Okay, okay, but straighten out the media, will you?"

Good negotiations are slow moving, lacking in action, and, in short, boring. The broadcast of false information and inflammatory speculation about impending tactical action is much more exciting —even if it is not true.

Live coverage of entry teams moving into position and sniper or observer teams has caused problems for negotiators and endangered, if not killed, hostages and tactical team personnel. Topics such as live coverage of tactical team members must be agreed upon with media representatives before media coverage heightens the crisis.

During a hostage situation in which radios were being used to talk to the subject, an officer approached the negotiator and said, "The media is listening to everything you guys are saying."

The negotiator said, " I figured they were, because of the radios."

The officer responded with, "No, I mean with shotgun microphones from over there."

"Over there" was approximately a block away. Standing around for hours, with not much happening, negotiators and officers will say things they do not really mean or, if they do mean it, they do not want to hear themselves saying it on the local 11 o'clock news show. The media often has much better equipment in terms of cameras and sound than does law enforcement.

A representative of the Federal Aviation Administration (FAA) should be on the negotiator's contact list and a working relationship established. Low-flying aircraft can cause real problems in an incident. FAA can designate the airspace above the crisis site as restricted. Any pilots who fly into the restricted airspace do so at the risk of their licenses.

The multitude of media personnel who arrive at a major crisis can get in the way of crisis management team members. Across the street from one major 11-day incident, rooftops that provided a better camera angle for the media were renting for $500.00 per day.

It is recommended that negotiators do not put "Negotiator" on the back of raid jackets because of the media attention that it will draw to the negotiator. One negotiator said he had the word put on the back of his jacket so his snipers would know who he was. It is further recommended that if negotiators are that concerned about snipers, they do not go forward.

Given the opportunity, the media will tie up the subject's telephone line. It is a good idea to have representatives of the local telephone company on the negotiator's contact list. Usually, they can change the subject's telephone number quickly so that only the telephone company and negotiators will know the number. Depending on the local equipment, they will be able to assist negotiators in any number of ways; talk to them before the crisis arises. Demanding a meeting with a telephone company security representative at 4:00 a.m. during an incident is not the way to establish a good working relationship.

It is also a good idea to have the negotiation and tactical team leader review any press releases before they are distributed or announcements are made. If the subject has access to radio or television, nothing should be said that would disrupt the negotiation or tactical effort.

Use of Third-Party Intermediaries

Third-party intermediaries are non-law enforcement personnel, including family, friends, attorney, clergy, mental health professionals, media, and others. Even law enforcement officers might be regarded as third-party intermediaries if they are being used primarily because of a previously established personal relationship, as opposed to a professional relationship, with the subject.

Since the inception of hostage negotiation teams in the early 1970s, negotiation trainers have generally discouraged the use of third-party intermediaries (TPI). However, despite their training to the contrary, negotiators have often used TPIs because sometimes they work. Sometimes the use of TPIs results in a disaster. Knowing when TPIs will be helpful and when they will be hurtful is the dilemma for negotiators and crisis managers.

Frustration at the lack of apparent progress seems to be a major reason for using TPIs despite previous training and the known risks involved. There will often be friends and relatives of the subject on scene insisting that they can talk him out with no problem. Negotiators should be asking themselves, if this person is such a powerful influence on the subject why did he not go to them in the first place, rather than do what he is doing now?

A negotiator related the story of a domestic incident where the husband had a gun to his wife's head and raged on about her for hours. As time dragged on, his rage did not appear to be diminishing. Meanwhile, a man describing himself as "a friend of the family" was on-scene and insisting that he could resolve the situation for negotiators. Finally, after many hours, they put the "friend" on the telephone. Almost immediately, two shots were heard. The man shot and killed his wife and himself. The "friend" negotiators had put on the telephone was having an affair with the wife and their affair was the reason for the incident. Negotiators rarely have all of the pertinent information.

A patrol officer observed a man on the 10th-story balcony of a high-rise hotel on the beach of a popular vacation destination. The man was perched on the railing, hanging out into space. Initially, things were going well, but then the officer sent the man's wife out onto the balcony. The first words out of her mouth were, "Harry, you've been doing this ridiculous nonsense for the past 20 years and I'm getting fed up with it."

The officer, realizing that the situation was not developing the way he had intended, pulled her back into the hotel room. The couple had a teenage son who seemed to be a stable young man and he was sent out onto the balcony. His unfortunate first words were, "Hey, Pop, you sure are screwing up our vacation." With those words, the man let go and fell 10 stories to his death.

An officer, out on patrol, found a young man in a cemetery with a gun to his head. The officer and his backup offered the young man a soft drink in return for a bullet. The young man agreed and he was given a drink. The young man then reached into his pocket, retrieved one of nearly 50 rounds, and gave it to the officers. The trade sounded fair to him.

As it happened, the subject had just broken up with his girlfriend, so officers had her brought to the scene. She was permitted to speak to the subject and cried, "You wimp. This is exactly why I broke up with you. You do wimpy stuff like this."

The subject responded with, "Wimp, huh?" and shot himself through the head. Threatened suicides are emotional situations. The negotiator's objective should be to decrease the emotional factor.

In another incident, when there had been no apparent progress over 10 hours with a barricaded, borderline psychotic subject who had been shooting at passersby, the police were frustrated. Throughout that time, the subject's brother, who was on scene, insisted that he could resolve the incident in five minutes if the police would just allow him to speak to his brother. That turned out to be true, although, tragically, not in the manner the brother had intended. For, when the police finally relented, the subject's brother peered around a corner of the building and was immediately shot through the head by the subject. When the police called out, "Hey, you just shot your brother," the distraught subject came charging out. He was tackled and subdued.

Using third-party intermediaries can result in any number of problems. Consider the following:

- **Ethical considerations may impede or prevent progress**. The ethics of mental-health professionals, the clergy, the media, attorneys, and others, are going to be different from those of law enforcement. For example, negotiators have no ethical problem with lying for the greater good of the incident, or they may participate in the tactical resolution of the incident. Both of these examples might be an ethical concern for some professions. Law enforcement procedures and objectives can put persons in other professions in a very difficult ethical position.

- **Under stress, TPIs might respond inappropriately.** Despite the best intentions, negotiators cannot expect them to respond to a stressful incident the way an experienced negotiator or officer would.
- **TPIs are not trained negotiators.** Crisis negotiation is an art taught to police. Another professional may be trained and even an expert in his own field. However, few people outside of law enforcement get an opportunity to see the things a law enforcement officer sees and responds to on a near-daily basis.
- **TPIs are not used to violence.** Something that law enforcement officers see that persons in other professions do not see is violence. Police are often there when violence is occurring or immediately afterward. Counseling and therapy professionals do not generally perform their services when the person is in crisis, with gun in hand and threatening violence or suicide. Their ministrations are conducted under entirely different circumstances. By the time they meet the subject, the precipitating event has long since passed, he has calmed down, and he has something to gain by presenting a front that the negotiator never saw.
- **TPIs are not familiar with police procedures and tactics.** Again, even with the best of intentions, TPIs can say something to the subject that causes law enforcement a problem. For example, they may blurt out something that is not to the tactical advantage of law enforcement. They do not understand that negotiators work closely with tactical teams before they make any statements that may affect the tactical effort.
- **TPIs cause law enforcement to lose control.** Once law enforcement responds to an incident, its management becomes their responsibility. Once they start using TPIs, they have effectively lost control.
- **The subject's response to intermediary is unknown.** It is very difficult to predict the subject's response to TPIs even

if they have successfully fulfilled that role previously. In one situation, the subject's mother was successfully used, talking him into surrendering in a short period of time. The subject, some time later, took a hostage for the second time. His mother was again brought in by law enforcement. This time, the man committed suicide.

- **TPIs will not have the same perspective as law enforcement.** Persons in other professions, by training and experience, will not have the same outlook as law enforcement. Reporters will see the incident as a story. Mental health professionals will tend to view the subject as a patient. Parents will view the subject as their child.

The subject's family members can present special problems. They often show up on scene insisting that they can talk the subject out. Remember though, that they bring their emotional baggage into a situation. They may feel the subject is embarrassing the family. They may feel guilt over something they said or did or did not say or do. Too often in law enforcement there has been an unfortunate assumption that a good family relationship exists.

In one incident, the subject's mother and sister arrived on scene. Independently, they were asked what could be said to get the subject to surrender. Both said essentially the same thing, "Nothing. I suggest you shoot the son of a bitch." Not the advice negotiators were hoping for.

Family values are also hard to predict. In one long situation, the subject's sister arrived on scene. After a careful briefing and debriefing, she was put on the telephone with the subject. The first words out of her mouth were, "Hang in there. The whole family is really proud of you."

Sometimes there appears to be an assumption that the subject's background is similar to the negotiator's past. In one protracted siege, the negotiator offered to put the female subject's father on the telephone and she immediately began screaming and hung up on the negotiator. The woman's sister, who was nearby, said, "Boy, you shouldn't have mentioned Daddy."

The negotiator said, "Yeah, but why?"

The sister said, "Well, he raped her when she was little and she's never forgiven him for that."

The family dynamics are never fully known to the negotiator. The TPI's perception of the relationship may differ from the subject's. Introducing family members brings in additional factors that complicate the incident psychologically. Negotiators want to keep issues to a minimum and keep things simple.

In incidents that are emotionally charged, as in spontaneous sieges, it is especially dangerous to use TPIs. In deliberate and anticipated sieges, the subject is far less emotional and the risk of using TPIs would not appear to be as great as it is in spontaneous sieges. In fact, the emotion negotiators are injecting into deliberate and anticipated sieges by using TPIs may be helpful while not emotionally overloading the subject.

The "Boss" as Negotiator

Negotiators are not decision-makers. In some agencies, however, the negotiator is permitted limited authority to grant relatively small requests for cigarettes and other minor items. This limited authority gives negotiators some latitude to exercise their judgment. In general though, the negotiator acts as a middleman between the subject and command.

An old negotiation maxim goes, "Negotiators don't command and commanders don't negotiate." In any kind of negotiation, negotiators should not be the final authorities or portray themselves as the final authority for a variety of reasons. Before any deals or decisions are made, the negotiator wants to confer with others to ensure that the situation has not changed. While the negotiator has been talking to the subject, things have been happening, information is being gathered, personnel may have been rotated, etc.

A concern about on-scene commanders acting as negotiators is the loss of their objectivity. If lower-ranking negotiators become too emotionally involved, they can easily be replaced. If on-scene commanders, who are also the ranking persons on scene, become too emotionally involved, even informing them of suspicions can be problematic.

On-scene commanders are in charge of the entire crisis management effort. Commanders cannot split their time by being both a commander and a negotiator. Neither can they also be tactical team leaders, intelligence gatherers, detectives, public information officers, and electronics technicians. If commanders are on the telephone negotiating with the subject, they are neglecting the command of the rest of the crisis management effort.

Stalling for time is the primary tactic of negotiators—especially in spontaneous sieges. If it becomes obvious to the subject the commander is stalling for time, it will be very difficult to maintain rapport with the subject. Stalling for time can be difficult for any negotiator, but if the person in charge is stalling, it is even more difficult.

Street experience is an important attribute of a negotiator. If the on-scene commander is lacking in recent street experience, rapport building may be difficult. Unfortunately, the lack of street experience or even law enforcement experience and training has also been deadly for some law enforcement executives.

In many jurisdictions, especially in rural areas, the chief law enforcement executive will delegate authority to manage "routine" incidents down to the sergeant or lieutenant level. Eventually, though, a major incident comes along and with the publicity, the chief or sheriff will take personal command even though he or she is not experienced or trained—a very dangerous combination for all involved.

Crisis Negotiation Team

The precise structure of a crisis negotiation team is based on local needs, resources, attitudes, personalities, skills, and talents. Reviewed here are the tasks that should be accomplished by someone on a crisis negotiation team. Before getting into specific team tasks, remember that crisis negotiation is a team effort and no matter what the size of your agency is, never negotiate alone. If there are no other trained negotiators readily available, a patrol officer should sit next to the negotiator. There should always be someone with whom a negotiator can confer.

In every incident, there is just one primary negotiator. In all cases, their main role is to act as intermediaries between their commanders and the subjects in an effort to optimize any opportunities for an arrest with minimum force, as required by law. In talking to the subjects, the primary negotiators also develop intelligence for both the negotiation and tactical efforts.

A secondary negotiator often has several jobs, the most important of which is to help the primary negotiator listen to the subject. Therefore, it is important that he or she monitor the negotiations and help the primary negotiator by providing topics for discussion.

Another critically important task that often falls upon secondary negotiators is maintaining a log of all negotiation events with the time of the event. During a negotiation, negotiators sometimes have the feeling that they do not need to write events down because they will never forget. In the heat of battle, they do forget. Crisis negotiators should document everything because they may need to reconstruct events in court and that is very difficult without a log.

Secondary negotiators provide emotional support to primary negotiators. A pat on the back, a thumbs-up signal, or going on a break with primary negotiators can do wonders for their stress levels. Secondary negotiators are also available to relieve the primary negotiators if that need should arise. Generally, secondary negotiators are the most tuned in to what is happening in the negotiation process and they are the logical same-shift replacement for primary negotiators.

Negotiation team leaders monitor the negotiations and act as liaison with on-scene commanders and tactical team leaders. They suggest tactics and strategy, and give other advice to primary negotiators. In some law enforcement agencies, a senior, experienced negotiator who is known and respected by commanders and tactical personnel fills this role.

It is best not to be whispering to primary negotiators as they are attempting to listen to the subject. No one can listen to two people at the same time and it is vitally important that the negotiator be listening to the subject. There is also the possibility that the subject may overhear what is being whispered to the primary and the primary is going to lose credibility—or worse.

The best negotiation course for a primary negotiator is to meet with the rest of the negotiation team between contacts with the subject. In these meetings, the team should fully discuss what will be said, how it will be said and the subject's likely response to what the negotiator says. When contact is made, primaries go with the team strategy as best they can. If subjects bring up a topic that has not been discussed, as is likely, it may be best for primary negotiators to tell subjects that they will have to get back to them on that topic.

While primary negotiators are actively talking to the subject, the most common form of communication is via notes being passed from the secondary to the primary. All notes should flow through the secondary negotiator to the primary. Some negotiation teams put the time on each note and, after the primary reads it, the note is put on a spindle. This procedure establishes a rough log of events, although it is not a substitute for a full log. A danger in using notes is that, in the heat of battle, the primary might just read a note from the secondary aloud to the subject without reading it first.

During an incident, there should be an ongoing intelligence-gathering effort. There should be a debriefing of responding officers, neighbors, friends, relatives, spouses, witnesses, employers, and anyone else who has pertinent information. The information gathered should be coming to a designated person on the crisis negotiation team. This intelligence support person provides the information to the team and posts it on the situation boards.

Some teams appoint a resource person, who essentially runs errands for the team. This person gets everything the team needs, ranging from miscellaneous information to coffee.

A tactical liaison person can be an important component on a crisis negotiation team. Usually, the tactical liaison person is someone who has had tactical team experience. This person channels crucial information between the tactical team and negotiators, especially when timing is critical. For example, if the tactical team is at their entry point and the subject discovers their presence, this information needs to get to the entry team immediately. The quickest way to pass along this information is to have direct communication between the negotiators and the entry team.

The tactical liaison person listens to the negotiation for information that is of specific use to the tactical team. Negotiators are trained to know that they can provide this service but in the stress of negotiation, intelligence can be overlooked or negotiators may not even be aware that the tactical team could use a particular piece of information.

Be aware though, that some commanders do not like negotiators to talk directly to the tactical team. Their concern is that the negotiators and tactical personnel will leave them out of the loop by making decisions without their approval. It is the negotiation and tactical team leaders' jobs to ensure that commanders are kept informed.

Mental-health professionals (MHPs) provide a variety of services to the crisis negotiation team. While they do not negotiate, they do assess the mental state of the subject and recommend negotiation techniques and approaches to the team. They can also render emotional and stress-management support to the negotiation team.

In fairness to them, any MHP working with a negotiation team should receive negotiation training before becoming a member of the negotiation team. Crisis negotiation is not something learned in graduate school. MHPs need time to work out how their experience can be most useful to the team's needs. They also need time to learn what their role will be in a crisis situation, and there may also be some ethical dilemmas for them to work out for themselves.

It would be difficult to overstate the importance of getting all crisis management personnel working together as a team. At a minimum, a team's members include tactical, negotiation, and command personnel. Others requiring training might include patrol officers and road deputies, anyone with specialized skills such as electronics technicians, persons on the negotiators' contact list, public information officers, persons searching databases for information on the subject, dispatchers, and many others. In the words of Casey Stengel, "It's easy to get the players. Gettin' em to work together, that's the hard part."

Supplies and Equipment for Ready Kit

The more that can be accomplished before the crisis, the less negotiators will have to do during its run. It is worthwhile to set aside items that negotiators know they might need during an incident. The articles in a ready kit will depend on locality, weather, resources, and other variables. It is extremely difficult to be "warm and fuzzy" with someone when the negotiator is soaked to the skin, cold, and being eaten by mosquitoes. It helps to be creative before arriving on scene. Listed below are some typical items in a ready kit:

- Box with activity logs, situation reports, pens, stick-on notes, 5x8 index cards, magic markers, lined tablets, reference materials, notes, hostage-debriefing protocols

- Battery powered clock
- Tape recorder with extra batteries, jacks for headphones, speakers, fresh tapes, extension cord
- Video and still camera with film and tape
- Bullhorn
- Battery-operated flashlight or reading light
- Raid jacket
- Body armor
- Package-wrapping or butcher paper with masking tape or thumb tacks for situation boards
- Foul-weather gear, hat, and sunglasses
- Aspirin and antacid
- List of contacts and resources to be checked
- Insect repellent and sunscreen
- A physician's desk reference or other guide to medications (paperback editions are available)
- Bible to look up scriptural references
- Mirror on telescoping rod for looking around corners
- Specialty tools

The Tactical Role of the Negotiator

A crisis management team is just that, a team. As with all teams, to be effective, team players must train together on a regular basis. It follows then, that negotiators should train regularly with the tactical team. Training together not only leads to better timing during a crisis but personnel learn each other's job requirements and needs better. They also learn each other's attitudes, skills, talents, and personalities.

Intelligence gathering through direct dialogue with the subject is an important part of the negotiator's role. The negotiation process itself produces additional time for intelligence gathering. Negotiators, as a byproduct of the negotiation process, provide additional opportunities for intelligence gathering. The release of hostages provides an opportunity for intelligence gathering through the debriefing of former hostages. Agreements to deliver items allow for an approach to the crisis site and provide occasions for direct, closer observation and photographic surveillance.

The passage of time is important to the tactical team for the following reasons.

- It generates a period for the tactical team to develop and rehearse an emergency and deliberate-assault plan.
- Prolonged negotiation might lead to the subject's developing a routine inside the crisis site that could be advantageous to the tactical team, in that they know what to expect of him at given times.
- An ongoing dialogue could aid a forced-entry or sniper option.
- Negotiators might provide a cover story for tactical movement.

A concern since the early days of hostage negotiation is whether a negotiation team should be told of an impending tactical entry. The specific concerns are that the negotiator might inadvertently—or even intentionally—reveal the upcoming team entry or sniper shot. A second concern is that the negotiator's emotional involvement could alter his objectivity to the point of somehow disrupting the tactical option. Both of these concerns, however, appear to be unsubstantiated. Over a period of years, FBI Academy crisis negotiation instructors asked thousands of negotiators all over the world if they knew of any case where the negotiator gave away a tactical action or became so emotionally involved that they disrupted tactical plans. Not a single case was reported.

Situation Boards

A situation board in its simplest form is a length of paper taped or tacked to a wall or even taped to the side of a patrol car. As information regarding the subject, victims, and siege location comes in, the intelligence-support person posts the new information in columns on the situation board. This information should be within view of the negotiators and continually updated. Anything of potential interest to negotiators should be posted. A typical situation board will have, as a minimum, columns as listed below.

- Subject's name, description, photograph, weapons, arrest record, mental health history, medical problems and/or injuries
- Hostage's name, description, photograph, medical problems, or injuries
- Demands
- Deadlines
- A floor plan, photographs of the crisis site
- Positive things done for the subject
- Topics to be avoided in the negotiation
- Pages of the log as they are completed

Negotiating the Non-Negotiable Situation

There may be situations that, at the outset, do not appear to be winnable via negotiations. However, negotiations should still be opened. The negotiation process allows time for the tactical team to prepare and time for the gathering of information. The intelligence-gathering process might lead to alternatives, tactical and otherwise, that were not considered early in the incident.

The passage of time provides an interval for experts to arrive. Experts means anyone with specialized knowledge, such as the subject's doctor, a mental health professional, or a technician who mighty be of assistance to the crisis management team.

The negotiation process also delays the subject's actions and diverts his attention from whatever negotiators do not want him to be doing. For example, while the subject is talking to the negotiator, he is less likely to be engaged in harassing or harming his victims or fortifying his location. Finally, through negotiation, the authorities might discover that what they thought was non-negotiable is negotiable after all.

The Surrender

A big part of a negotiator's job is to educate the subject on how to surrender. The most common form of siege is the spontaneous siege where, as the name suggests, there has been little, if any, planning. Even if there has been some planning, it is unlikely that the plan will include surrender. The subject might want to surrender but not know how to go about it. Part of a negotiator's job is to educate the subject as to how the surrender will happen. Several recommendations are listed below.

- Emphasize what the subject has to gain by coming out at this time.
- Minimize the damage that has already occurred to this point.
- Ask what assurances are needed.
- Discuss the arrest plan with the tactical team early in the incident.
- Describe to the subject what will be seen when he comes out.
- Keep the "surrender ritual" in mind.
- To facilitate the surrender, the negotiator might be required to suggest scenarios and talk the subject out systematically.
- Continue to say, "when you come out," not "if you come out."
- Never take the weapon from the subject's hand.
- If the subject is surrendering to the negotiator, the negotiator should carefully coordinate all movement with tactical personnel including snipers.

In the 1970s, when negotiators spoke of the surrender ritual they had two scenarios in mind. In the first, the subject wants to surrender looking like a tough guy. For instance, in England, a subject was involved in a domestic dispute that negotiators were called upon to resolve. When the subject surrendered, the negotiator offered to put a sweater over the handcuffs so that the man's friends and neighbors waiting outside would not see them and cause the subject to be embarrassed. The subject said, "No, I want to go out with my fingers linked on top of my head just like in the American movies."

The second surrender ritual involved persons who wanted to come out looking like gentlemen. These individuals wanted to shower, shave, and change clothes before surrendering and appearing before television cameras. While these two forms of surrender ritual are still observed, negotiators have seen the surrender ritual take additional forms.

Another form of surrender ritual ends in the incident's just winding down. During two negotiated aircraft hijackings, food was provided in return for the release of a limited number of hostages. But, instead of 25 people coming off the plane, 40 came down the stairway. The stairway was left in place and passengers were just getting off the plane. The hijackers knew the incident was over and they merely let it die.

In another form of surrender ritual that has been observed, the subject allows himself to be "taken down" by the tactical team. In one such incident, the subject came out of his location to retrieve some food, and in another, he came out to turn off a light the authorities had refused to turn off. In both incidents, the subjects had to know the tactical team was there and that the tactical team would jump all over them when they came through the door. Now, as they sit in their respective cells and tell fellow inmates how they were captured, they can say, "An FBI S.W.A.T. team jumped me and there must have been five or 10 or 15 of them, but I got in some good licks before they got me."

He did not surrender. The S.W.A.T. team took him down. This ending to his incident puts him in a more "heroic" light to his fellow inmates than would meekly surrendering.

Before Deviating from Guidelines

With the understanding that crisis negotiation is an art rather than an exact science and that guidelines are not rules to be obeyed against good reason, the guidelines are often violated to meet the circumstances of a particular situation. Keep in mind, however, that crisis negotiation guidelines are the accumulated wisdom of many previous negotiators and should not be carelessly disregarded. The surest way of falling short in a liability lawsuit is to have ignored the guidelines in a losing effort.

At an FBI seminar, Lieutenant Anthony Hare, of the police department in Oakland, California, suggested the following if a guideline is to be broken:

- State the reason(s) for the guideline.
- State the risk(s) involved in deviating from the guideline.
- State why the deviation will be helpful.
- State how the negotiators will know if the deviation is working or failing.
- State a tentative plan for getting back on track or salvaging a failure.

The Effects of Negotiating on Negotiators

The effects of negotiating on negotiators can range from nonexistent to subtle to severe. An event that has a profound impact on one negotiator might not affect another. Even if negotiators have gone through many situations with no ill effects, there is no guarantee that they will be well after the next incident.

There is no wayto predict whether any one negotiator will have problems as a result of the negotiation process. Most do not have major problems, but some do. Few negotiations go off without a hitch and there are few negotiators who have not been distressed by some turn of events during a crisis. Many negotiators have remarked, for example, that the bad guy was easy but negotiating with their own boss during the incident was tough. Sometimes the negotiator's problem is for the duration of the incident, but sometimes the problem has longer-lasting effects.

Look out for the welfare of all negotiation team members. Discussed below are some of the problems encountered by negotiators.

Possible Short-Term Stressors and Problems

Identification with subject or victim is a source of stress and can be a problem. During a domestic situation, a sergeant acting as the negotiation team leader suddenly left the negotiation team's position and without authorization made entry into the subject's location. He arrested the subject without further incident. As it turned out, the family problems that had resulted in the siege were identical to those his family was facing.

Physical and psychological manifestations of anxiety can also be problematic. A wide range of physical symptoms has been observed. One negotiator, after being ordered to go face-to-face with a cop killer and doing so, said that he could not sit still for many hours afterward. Knowing he could not sleep, he walked to the station to do his report. He tried to do his report but was too restless so he walked home. When he arrived at home, he again could not sleep, so back to the station he went.

Another negotiator, who worked an incident that received national press coverage, said he was scheduled to give a presentation on negotiation the next day. When he attempted to give the presentation, his knees were still so weak that he had to conduct the entire presentation sitting down.

Negotiators have also reported nightmares, insomnia, and impotence for up to two weeks following an incident. Virtually every symptom seen in post-traumatic stress disorder has been observed among negotiators.

The most common psychological problem in the short run is a feeling of let-down. One negotiator said, "I'd been negotiating with this depressed guy all night. He had been crying and pouring out his story to me. At about hour 10, he went out onto the front porch and blew the top of his head off. We were a couple of houses up the block and could clearly hear the shot. At the sound, my lieutenant turned to me and said, 'Okay, that's it. Take a couple of hours off in the morning if you like.' How do you begin to tell your wife, girlfriend, boyfriend, or husband what has happened to you over that 10 hours? You can't."

Negotiators ride a high crest of adrenaline for hours and then, for better or worse, the incident is over—sometimes very suddenly. It is impossible to shut off the effects of adrenaline immediately. The adrenaline is still there, but the negotiator no longer needs it.

Among negotiators, isolation is a very common problem that has even been observed during exercises. Sometimes negotiators' body language will give them away, as they will turn their backs to the secondary negotiators. A negotiator who is attempting to isolate himself may say something like, "Leave me alone. Just give me a few more minutes with this guy. I can get him out if you will just leave me alone."

Frustrated negotiators have also been heard to say, "Let's just do it without telling the command post."

Negotiation team members, regardless of their frustration level, cannot isolate themselves from the commander or exceed their authority. The on-scene commander must be informed as to developments and the negotiation team's intentions.

In many situations, the first shift is too long and exhaustion on the part of negotiators can be become a problem. Exhaustion can lead to frustration, impulsivity, and poor judgment. The morning after a particularly grueling 16-hour shift, a negotiator said, "You know, it's amazing how that idea sounded so good last night and so bad today."

During incidents that extend into several days, mounting exhaustion becomes a particular problem. At the end of a long, stressful day, negotiators go home, go to bed, dream about the incident all night, and then go right back into it the next morning. It is almost as if they did not have a break. After several days of this routine, negotiators and other personnel are truly exhausted.

Possible Long-Term Stressors/Problems

Ego problems have been a recurring, troublesome problem for crisis negotiation teams as well as for individual negotiators. Some negotiators have become hometown heroes. When an incident occurs, the chief or sheriff says, "I don't want anybody talking to this guy but Negotiator X."

The bad guy says, "I'll only talk to that guy I saw on television last week, Negotiator X!"

Media people are asking, "Is Negotiator X here yet?"

Before long, Negotiator X begins thinking, "I'm the only person who can really handle these situations. It must be a gift from God!"

Any negotiators who assume too much credit for "wins" as well as too much blame for "losses" can cause problems for themselves, their teams, and their future negotiation efforts. Some negotiators have been removed from teams because their egos were out of control.

After developing a reputation as a negotiator, some negotiators start taking on command responsibilities. When on-scene commanders are no longer asking for recommendations but are looking to the negotiator to tell them what to do, the problems begin. Negotiators should never forget their limited role. Negotiators do not want the commander to negotiate and negotiators should remember to never act the role of commander.

Some negotiators become negotiation fanatics. Unquestionably, crisis negotiation is an interesting, exciting field and the more a negotiator knows about, it the better. Law enforcement officers are often accused of living their stressful jobs. Adding a preoccupation with negotiation to an already stressful lifestyle can only make things worse. Keep your job and your personal life in perspective.

Sometimes, despite a negotiation team's best effort, incidents do not end well. Some negotiators start reliving the incident or feeling guilty over things they feel that should have been said or done.

The best inoculation against feelings of responsibility over things that went wrong and guilt about the way things happened is to work and study. If negotiators can walk away from an incident feeling that they gave it their best effort, that is all that can be asked and that is all negotiators can do.

Chapter 7

Abnormal Psychology for Crisis Negotiators

Introduction

Reviewed in this chapter are the two most commonly diagnosed personality disorders, antisocial and borderline personality disorders.* Also to be reviewed are schizophrenic and major depressive episodes. The intent of this section is not to make a diagnostician of negotiators but to familiarize them with the common behavior of those with whom they will be negotiating. Further, diagnostic category is not of particular interest to negotiators. Negotiators are concerned with controlling a person's behavior regardless of the diagnostic label placed on them. Even if negotiators were capable of arriving at a correct diagnosis, a diagnosis does not help them control the subject's behavior. Taking on the role of diagnostician could even embarrass the negotiator in court one day.

A personality disorder is composed of personality traits that are constant and maladaptive, and cause impairment and personal distress. People with personality disorders rarely visit a mental-health professional (MHP) for treatment of their disorder. Though they are

---

* The diagnostic categories referenced in this chapter are based upon those in the *Diagnostic and Statistical Manual of Mental Disorders Fourth Edition* of the American Psychiatric Association.

frequently deep in personal and legal problems, they do not think of themselves as requiring the assistance of an MHP. In a sense, a personality disorder is more like a lifestyle than a disease.

A non-law enforcement seminar attendee was asking for further clarification of the antisocial personality and his view of the world. Knowing this student had a "lead foot" and four speeding tickets as evidence of her habit, the instructor asked if she had seen an MHP about her behavior. To which she replied, "No. Why?"

The instructor said, "Well, you continue to speed despite the fact that you have been caught at it on several occasions. Apparently, you do not feel as if the laws apply to you. You are angry about paying the fines though you readily admit you broke the law. You feel no guilt or remorse about having broken the law. You have not learned anything from being punished. You have recklessly disregarded your own safety and the safety of others. You lied to the officer when he stopped you though you knew the lie could easily be detected if he chose to pursue it. Sounds like antisocial behavior to me."

Not really, but antisocial people may feel the same way about far more serious crimes. People with personality disorders do not believe that they have a problem. It is the rest of world that has it all wrong.

Antisocial Personality Disorder

When new to the FBI, an agent was assigned to the office fugitive squad. He participated in the arrest of a fugitive who had committed four homicides and possibly several more. One of the subject's victims, who had survived his assault, telephoned the FBI one afternoon and said that the subject was coming back to town. The fugitive had telephoned her and said he wanted to talk to her. She feared that he was not coming back to talk to her but to kill her.

She had ample reason to be concerned. In his assault, he had slashed her face with a knife, leaving wounds that required 200 stitches to repair the damage. He had sliced off her left ear but surgeons had sewed it back on. Finally, he had cut off her left breast. Now, he wanted to "talk."

She told the FBI that he would be arriving at the city bus terminal and provided the details of his arrival. The FBI arrived at the bus terminal with 17 agents to ensure that once he was in the terminal there would be no way out. They had every possible exit covered by several agents. When the subject entered the terminal they took him down, frisked him, handcuffed him, and took him to the FBI office for interview.

During the interview, the agent was shocked, saying that perhaps because he was so new to law enforcement that he still expected "bad guys" to look like the bad guys he had seen on television and in the movies. This subject was nothing at all like what he had expected. This bad guy was well dressed and well groomed, charming, articulate, a "nice" guy, and yet, a serial killer. In short, he was an antisocial personality and astonishing in the incongruity.

The reader has possibly studied the antisocial personality in high school, college, or the police academy, when these individuals were known as sociopaths or psychopaths. For our purposes, these will be treated as the same disorder.

Characteristics

Persons suffering from antisocial personality disorder tend to lack empathy. They are often cold, cynical, and scornful of the feelings, rights, and suffering of others. Some believe that this pattern begins in childhood, perhaps as early as age eight or nine, or in the early teens.

He may have an inflated opinion of himself to the point of arrogance, despite his lack of experience or training in a particular field. He may be unemployed because he insists that he will take only a supervisory position, for example. He is cocky and self-assured with little legitimate reason to be so.

He often possesses a glib, superficial charm that he will use to his advantage in a variety of situations, including those with the opposite sex, potential employers, and victims. Sometimes this individual will use technical terms to impress someone unfamiliar with a topic. He may, however, experience unpleasant moods, including complaints of tension, boredom, and depression. As do many persons suffering from personality disorders, he tends to be impulsive.

He is irresponsible and exploitative in personal relationships and may have a history of many sexual partners. In fact, he may never have sustained a monogamous relationship. If a parent, he will be irresponsible in this relationship as well.

Common backgrounds include less-than-honorable discharges from the military services, failure to be self-supporting, impoverishment, or even homelessness, and he may have spent many years in prison. He is more likely than are those in the general population to die by violent means. Childhood backgrounds include abuse or neglect, unstable or erratic parenting, and inconsistent parental discipline.

Common Behaviors

When one considers the lifestyle of someone with an antisocial personality, it becomes evident why they often find themselves in jail or prison. They repeatedly con others for profit or just for the "fun" of it, with little thought to the future. They may be impulsive, irritable, and aggressive, as indicated by repeated verbal or physical assaults.

Their reckless indifference regarding their own safety and the safety of others is reflected in driving records that may include multiple speeding citations, drunk-driving arrests, and multiple accidents. Their recklessness may extend to engaging in high-risk sex and drug abuse.

Antisocial personalities are unwavering in their path of irresponsibility in all facets of their lives. Their work and financial histories are a shambles. They might abruptly quit showing up for work and have no plans for future employment. They might also be unemployed even when jobs are readily available. Further evidence of irresponsibility can be indicated by failure to pay debts or child support, or support other dependents on a regular basis.

They may be indifferent to having hurt, abused, or otherwise mistreated someone else. In fact, they may blame the victim for being stupid or for deserving what they got. After being arrested on a rape charge, they might say something like, "What was she thinking walking out on the street at that hour? If I didn't rape her, somebody else would have. She deserved what she got for being so dumb. She was just asking for it."

Communication Suggestions

- Keep the subject's egocentricity in mind, as people with antisocial personalities do everything out of self-interest.

- Keep the subject busy to preclude harassment of his victims or hostages.
- The subject must be convinced that the safe release of the hostages is to his advantage because of his self-serving behavior.
- Do not try to "con" this con man about how easily he is going to avoid punishment because he knows the system.
- It is unlikely that girlfriends, wives, or other family members will be of value as third party intermediaries because he generally cares little about these relationships.

Borderline Personality Disorder

This disorder is the second most commonly diagnosed personality disorder after the antisocial personality disorder. The occurrence in the general population is about 2%. These individuals are described as "borderline" because they are borderline psychotic, especially during times of stress.

Some MHPs have reported that if they are interviewing patients and they find, within 10 minutes, that they hate them, they are often diagnosed as suffering from borderline personality disorder. Corrections officers seem to be able to recognize this type of individual faster than officers or deputies, perhaps because they interact with them on a daily basis. Police officers appear to view people with a borderline personality disorder as just another troublesome, difficult citizen having a bad day. Corrections officers, who live among them, know that they are not just having a bad day. What the police officer is observing on any particular day is the way these people are every day.

A negotiator reported that during the course of a negotiation, a prison inmate hostage taker lifted his tee shirt. The man's chest was a mass of scars. When the negotiator asked what had happened to him, the negotiator was told that the inmate would cut pieces of meat off his chest and mail it to people. By the inmate's reckoning, the recipient was challenged to send a bigger piece of meat back. If the recipient did not send a bigger piece back, the recipient was not as "macho" as the inmate.

This inmate was a large, bisexual male who had been involved in a number of extremely volatile homosexual relationships while in prison and who had assumed the male role with two inmate "queens" at the time of the incident. According to prison officials, he had mutilated his body with knife cuts on multiple occasions to "prove" his love to his homosexual lovers. The aforementioned man was diagnosed as suffering from borderline personality disorder.

In one extreme example of self-mutilation, when the warden was new to the penitentiary, the inmate cut off one of his own testicles and threw it at the warden. Presumably, he was challenging the warden to throw two testicles back. Not surprisingly, he did not.

Characteristics

- Persons with borderline personality disorder may undermine themselves as they near a goal. They might, for example, drop out of school just before graduation or quit a good job just when it starts to look good. Corrections officers report that these individuals will get into trouble at exactly the worst time, such as just before release.
- Suicide, with a completion rate of 8%–10%, is more prevalent than in the general population.
- Physical handicaps resulting from self-inflicted injuries and failed suicide attempts are common. Corrections personnel report that many borderline personalities often have self-inflicted scars all over their bodies that are referred to as "battle scars." One corrections officer reported that a borderline personality had sliced open his chest and packed it with feces in the hope that if his wound did not kill him, the infection would.
- The impairment from the disorder and the risk of suicide recede with advancing age, as do the recurring suicidal behavior, gestures, threats, or self-mutilating behavior.
- These individuals may experience psychotic-like behavior during times of stress.
- They may feel more secure with a pet or inanimate object than in interpersonal relationships.
- Recurrent job losses, interrupted education, and broken marriages are common.
- Childhood histories may include physical and sexual abuse, neglect, familial conflict, and early parental loss or separation.

Course

There is considerable variability in the course of this disorder. The most common pattern is one of chronic instability in early adulthood and milder manifestations of the disorder as the person advances in age.

Familial Pattern

The disorder is five times more common among close relatives of those with the disorder than in the general population.

Common Behaviors

- People with borderline personality disorder often exhibit frenzied efforts to avoid real or imagined abandonment. They can barely tolerate being alone and fear abandonment or rejection. This fear may be the reason for self-mutilating behavior and suicidal gestures. To them, abandonment implies that they have been "bad."
- Borderline personalities may experience a pattern of unstable and intense relationships characterized by alternating between extremes of idealization and devaluation. They may idealize lovers, for example, on a first or second meeting, demand a lot of time together, and share the most intimate details of their lives early in a relationship. Very soon, however, they may feel that the other person does not care enough, does not give enough, or is not there enough. It has been suggested that these emotional extremes may be at the root of a significant number of domestic situations worked by negotiators.
- They may also undergo identity disturbances, that is, experience an unstable self-image or sense of self. Examples of this experience include sudden and dramatic shifts in self-image, characterized by shifting goals, values, and vocational aspirations. There may be sudden changes in opinions and plans about career, sexual identity, values, and types of friends. Their usual self-image is based on good or evil.

- Borderline people can be impulsive in at least two areas that are potentially self-damaging. Examples of their impulsivity might include sprees and binges of virtually any kind including gambling, spending money irresponsibly, unsafe sex, substance abuse, reckless driving, and binge eating.
- Their mood is basically unstable and unpleasant most of the time. This unpleasant mood is frequently spiked with periods of anger, panic, or despair.
- Chronic feelings of emptiness are commonplace, as these people are easily bored and may be constantly seeking something to do.
- Their inappropriate, intense anger or difficulty controlling their anger results in outbursts of temper and recurrent physical fights. They may display extreme sarcasm, bitterness, or verbal outbursts. Anger is seen when a lover, for example, is depicted as neglectful, withholding, uncaring, or abandoning. Afterward, they express shame and guilt over their behavior. They view their own outbursts as evidence of their evil ways.
- Sometimes borderline personalities will under go transient, stress-related feelings of suspiciousness or the belief that they are being harassed, persecuted, or treated unfairly.

In differentiating between antisocial and borderline, the borderline will:

- Have a history of suicide attempts
- Express self-loathing
- Have intense, ambivalent attachments where antisocials will have few or none
- Have more conscience
- Be far more emotional

Communication Suggestions

- Use active listening techniques, particularly emotion labeling, to build rapport, defuse emotionality, and gather intelligence.
- Stay "with" the subject as much as possible to preclude him/her from doing something impulsively.
- Be alert for clues to suicide or homicide.

- Reassure the subject that help is available and that you will help find it.
- Be prepared for displays of and shifts in emotionality.
- Be extremely careful about allowing friends and relatives to speak directly to the subject during an incident.

Schizophrenia

It was 3:00 p.m. and Rose sat on a bench at a major airport carefully studying security procedures. After watching for a while, she realized that she could never get through security with the revolver she had shoved in her coat pocket. Rose wondered how she was going to board an airplane. She had to go. After all, Prince Charles and Muhammad Ali were after her. Just that morning she saw a sign that told her to leave the country.

Rose noticed that arriving passengers were coming through a nearby door. Only one woman, who often turned her back and did not appear to be particularly watchful, was guarding this door. Going through this exit appeared to be her best opportunity. If she was lucky, she could slip through this door while the woman's back was turned. Rose braced herself, then tried it when the woman turned her back to the door.

As she slipped through, the guard turned once again and saw her. The guard attempted to stop her and Rose pulled her gun. She had to go. The guard tried to take Rose's gun but it discharged and she shot the guard. Rose boarded a plane that had passengers already on board.

Soon, airport security personnel were calling out to her and telling her that they only wanted to talk. After they talked, Rose could go home. Rose knew they were lying. She had just shot somebody.

Later, an FBI negotiator began talking to Rose and she liked him until she realized he was just stalling for time. Rose knew that the FBI and police needed time to set up their command post and get tactical teams in place. Rose's problems were mounting. Prince Charles was standing right next to the negotiator, so there was no need to tell him about the Prince and Muhammad Ali.

After several hours of negotiation, a tactical team boarded the aircraft in an attempt to apprehend Rose, but she was a large woman and there was a struggle. Rose was finally restrained only after being shot in the shoulder. She had been diagnosed as a paranoid schizophrenic at an early age and was later confined to a mental-health facility for an indefinite period as a result of the shooting and aircraft hijacking attempt.

Schizophrenia is a serious mental illness that affects about 2.5 million Americans, usually between the ages of 15 to 25. Persons who are diagnosed with paranoid schizophrenia develop it somewhat later in life than persons with other forms of the disease.

Among the public there is often confusion that seems to originate with the word "schizophrenia" itself. Although schizophrenia literally means, "split mind," people with the disorder do not have a split or multiple personality. Instead, they experience a "split" or loss of contact with reality. Further, this loss of contact with reality does not mean that they do not know what is going on around them. They can be incredibly sensitive to what is going on around them. Never confuse schizophrenia with being stupid.

There are five forms of schizophrenia—the paranoid type, disorganized type, catatonic type, undifferentiated type, and the residual type. In a study of hostage takers, the undifferentiated type was the most common, followed by the paranoid type.

Definitions

Schizophrenics encountered in hostage situations may be suffering from hallucinations or delusions that are defined as follows:

- Hallucinations are a sensory perception that occurs without an external stimulus. Hallucinations may occur in any of the senses, i.e., auditory, visual, tactile, smell, or taste. Hallucinations are generally unpleasant.
  1. Auditory hallucinations are the most common. Auditory hallucinations will be voices or sounds that can appear to be coming from inside or outside the head. The content of the hallucinations will be unpleasant and either talking to each other or commenting on the subject's thoughts or behaviors.
  2. Visual hallucinations is seeing things that are not there, such as giant bugs crawling all over a wall.

3. Tactile hallucinations are not uncommon among cocaine addicts, who may scratch bleeding wounds in their arms in an attempt to rid themselves of "coke bugs" crawling beneath their skin.
4. Gustatory hallucinations involve tasting things that are not there, such as poison in the person's food.
5. Olfactory hallucinations involve smelling things that are not present, such as decaying bodies.

- Delusions are a fixed, false belief that is held despite obvious evidence to the contrary. Listed below are several forms of delusion:
  1. Delusional jealousy is the delusion that one's sexual partner is being unfaithful.
  2. Erotomania is the delusion that another person, usually of higher status, is in love with the individual. This delusion involves feelings of love more than a sexual fantasy.
  3. Grandiose delusions are delusions of inflated worth, power, knowledge, identity, or special relationship to a deity or famous person.
  4. Delusions of being controlled involve a delusion in which feelings, impulses, thoughts, or actions are experienced as being under the control of some external force. There are three relatively common forms of thought control: (1) Thought broadcast is the delusion that everyone around a person can hear what the person is thinking. (2) Thought insertion is the delusion that thoughts are being inserted into the person's head in an almost physical way. (3) Thought withdrawal is the delusion that thoughts are being pulled out of a person's head in an almost physical way.
  5. A delusion of reference is a delusion whose theme is that events, objects, or other persons in one's immediate environment are related to one's self. For example, a high school student who was studying MacBeth told her teacher that the witches in the play were talking about her, personally. She said that she was evil and deserved to die. She was later diagnosed as being bipolar.
  6. Delusions of persecution are delusions in which the central theme is that the person is being attacked, harassed, cheated, persecuted, or conspired against.

Associated Features

Almost any symptom can occur as an associated feature including:

- Perplexed or disheveled appearance
- Eccentric dress
- Brief, concrete responses to questions
- Ritualistic, stereotyped behavior associated with magical thinking
- Depression, anxiety, or anger

Age of Onset

For schizophrenics in general, onset is usually during adolescence or early adulthood, but the disorder may begin in middle or late adult life. Paranoid schizophrenics, specifically, begin to exhibit behaviors in their 30s rather than in their teens or 20s. The onset of the disease is rare after age 50.

Impairment

There will be impairment in several areas of routine daily functioning, such as in jobs, social relations, and self-care. The impairment may be to the point of requiring supervision to meet the minimal standards of hygiene and safety. The organization of thinking, behavior, and emotional responsiveness often remains better preserved in the paranoid schizophrenic than in other forms of schizophrenia. In some ways, this relative lack of impairment in the paranoid schizophrenic allows them to plan, prepare, and carry out more-complex crimes such as an aircraft hijacking.

Complications

There is now somewhat controversial evidence indicating that these individuals are more violent than the general population. Their life expectancy is reduced due to an increased suicide rate and death from a variety of other causes including long-term poor hygiene.

A problem that has arisen on several occasions is the pathological fear of homosexuality on the part of some paranoid schizophrenics.

Some MHPs report that opposite-sex therapists are sometimes more effective with paranoid schizophrenics. The same should perhaps be considered when choosing negotiators.

Negotiators worked a barricade situation where the subject was convinced that his neighbor was a homosexual and attempting to seduce him. The subject fired at the totally unsuspecting neighbor's home.

Another negotiator was working very effectively with a schizophrenic. He had taken several hostages at a hospital where his son had died. The subject believed that he knew the reason for his son's illness and he had the cure but no one would listen to him. The subject was ready to walk out the door to surrender when a male doctor approached him from behind, put his hand on the subject's shoulder and said, "I love you. Let's do it together."

The subject went into a fury and said that God had spoken to him when the doctor touched his shoulder. He said that God warned him about death awaiting him on the other side of the door. He did not surrender.

At a forensic hospital, a schizophrenic awaiting evaluation attacked a lieutenant working the night shift. He later accused the lieutenant and captain of misting his bunk with "homosexual spray" in an attempt to turn him into a homosexual. It might be helpful to remember that paranoid schizophrenics also have a problem in relating to authority.

A paranoid schizophrenic brutally killed a man he thought was trying to seduce him. He refused to talk to male detectives but readily confessed to female detectives. Soon after getting out of prison on the first murder, he killed again. On the second occasion, the male victim was wearing shorts and the murderer considered the shorts to be a sexual come-on.

Personality Prior to the Illness

Before the onset of the disorder, persons are generally described as suspicious, introverted, withdrawn, eccentric, or impulsive.

Predisposing Factors

Scientists do not know what causes the illness but research suggests that problems with brain chemistry and structure may be responsible.

Prevalence

The prevalence of schizophrenia is usually estimated to be between 0.5% and 1%.

Sex Ratio

The disorder is apparently equally common in both sexes, though there might be a higher rate among males. However, women are more likely to have a later onset, have more noticeable mood symptoms, and a better prognosis.

Course

The prodromal phase is the time period during which the person is sliding into the disease. Prodromes are symptoms indicating the onset of a disease. During this phase there is a clear deterioration from a previous level of functioning. It is characterized by social withdrawal, impairment in role functioning, peculiar behavior, neglect of personal hygiene and grooming, disturbances in communication, bizarre ideas, unusual perceptual experiences, and lack of initiative, interests, or energy. Friends and relatives often describe the behaviors as a change in personality or say that the individual is no longer "the same person."

During the active phase, psychotic behavior such as delusions and hallucinations are clearly noticeable.

The residual phase follows the active phase. Behaviors during this phase are similar to that of the prodromal phase, except that the impairment in role functioning tends to be more common in the residual phase. During this phase some of the psychotic behavior, such as delusions or hallucinations, may persist. A return to the person's original personality is not common. Residual impairment often increases between episodes during the initial years of the disorder.

Familial Pattern

There is a higher prevalence of the disorder in close relatives of people with schizophrenia than would be expected in the general population, though there is no agreement as to a single cause for the disease. There is no laboratory test for schizophrenia.

Treatment/Medication

Antipsychotic medications often decrease agitation and anxiety, and soften or stop hallucinations, but unrealistic beliefs change more slowly. Some medications often have some beneficial effects within hours of administration. There have not been many occasions where negotiators could get a schizophrenic to take medication during an incident. Many schizophrenics do not like to take their medication because of the side effects. Additionally, most medications do not work fast enough, especially on delusions, to be of assistance to negotiators.

Schizophrenics are sometimes seen with a cigarette in one hand and a can of soda in the other. One of the side effects of the medications given to schizophrenics is a feeling of "cotton" mouth. For that reason, officers may observe schizophrenics on medication walking around carrying something to drink. They also often carry a cigarette, because some schizophrenics report that smoking helps them to think clearly. As a practical matter for officers, it may not be a bad idea to offer a schizophrenic a cigarette and something to drink.

Common Behaviors

- The presence of hallucinations and delusions
- Functioning in such areas as work, social relations, and self-care markedly below the highest level achieved before the onset of the disturbance
- Marked social isolation or withdrawal and impairment in role functioning
- Peculiar behavior
- Impairment in personal hygiene and grooming
- Unusual speech patterns
  - Clanging—a speech pattern that strings rhyming words together
  - Word salad—a speech pattern that strings words with no apparent connection together
  - Neologisms—words made up by the person
  - Words out of context—common words but not used the way other persons use the word

In one hostage situation, the subject, who had been previously diagnosed and treated as a paranoid schizophrenic, would occasionally say a word or entire sentence backward and could do so with apparent ease. This speech pattern is not common.

- Odd beliefs or beliefs having no true cause may influence behavior
- Fascination with mechanical and electronic devices
- Unusual perceptual experiences
- Lack of initiative, interests, or energy
- Preoccupation with delusions or auditory hallucinations

Communication Suggestions

- The subject's need to explain might offer an opportunity to establish rapport.
- Do not try to argue the subject out of his delusions. The negotiator will not be able to talk schizophrenics out of their delusions and any attempt to do so will only make them angry. Neither should the negotiator say that they can see or hear things when they do not. If the subject asks the negotiator if he or she can see the hallucinated bugs, the negotiator should say, "No, I can't see them but I can understand that you do."
- Negotiators should not get into a schizophrenic's delusional system. Sometimes, negotiators may have to walk a narrow line to begin a dialogue. For example, schizophrenics might not talk to officers or negotiators unless they address the subject as "Princess." In this case, it might not be a bad idea to get into the delusional system to a minimal degree just to begin a dialogue.
- Try to ally yourself with the subject's perspective without sounding insincere.
- Avoid use of family members, as they may be part of the delusional system.
- Media attention might be a negotiable item.
- There could be a negative attitude toward the mental-health profession.
- Do not stare or get too close (expanded body space).

Remember that fear may be the underlying emotion in paranoid individuals.

Major Depressive Episode

An estimated 9 million Americans suffer from major depressive episodes (MDE). Approximately one in four women and one in 10 men will experience at least one debilitating episode of mood disorder in their lifetime.

Associated Features

- Tearfulness, anxiety, irritability, brooding, excessive concern with physical health, panic attacks, and phobias
- Difficulty is experienced in intimate relationships or sexual functioning.
- There may be marital, occupational, or academic problems.
- Alcohol or substance abuse is common.
- Increased use of medical services.
- Attempted or completed suicide.
- The suicide risk is especially high for individuals with a history of mental illness, previous suicide attempts, a family history of suicide, or current substance abuse. About 15% of the people with this disorder go on to commit suicide.
- Episodes often follow stressors such as childbirth or a loss of any kind.
- Sleep abnormalities are common in this group with 40%–60% of outpatients and up to 90% of inpatients having problems.

Culture and Gender Features

- Culture can influence the experience and communication of depression. In some cultures, depression may be experienced in terms of bodily symptoms rather than sadness or guilt. In hispanic and Mediterranean cultures people complain of "nerves" and headaches. In China, people say they are experiencing weakness, tiredness, or "imbalance."

- Women tend to report a worsening of symptoms several days before their periods.
- Depressive episodes occur twice as frequently in women as in men.

Course

- Symptoms of depression usually develop over days to weeks.
- The duration of an episode is also variable and, left untreated, may last six months or longer.
- In most cases, the behaviors completely disappear and the individual returns to the premorbid level. However, in about 20%–30% of cases some depressive behaviors can persist for months or years.

Common Behaviors

- People suffering from MDE will describe their moods as depressed, sad, hopeless, discouraged, or "down in the dumps." Many individuals report irritability, persistent anger, angry outbursts, or exaggerated frustration over minor matters. MDE is much more serious and should not be confused with the passing feelings of unhappiness we all experience from time to time. MDE is a "whole body" illness that can last for months or even years.
- MDE will often result in diminished interest or pleasure in usual activities.
- People feel less interested in hobbies or just don't care anymore. Some depressed people may not realize that they are depressed. They just feel tired and get worse and worse. A man may not realize, for example, that though he usually went fishing a couple of times a week, he has not gone fishing in the last month.

    A negotiator was working with a depressed, suicidal, barricaded subject. The negotiator, at a loss for something to say, saw the subject's bass boat in the backyard. With the thought that fishing might be something they could talk about, the negotiator asked the subject about fishing and the

boat. The subject's only response was that he had not been fishing for more than a month.
- In some people, there is a significant reduction in sexual interest.
- In children and adolescents, the mood may be irritable rather than sad.
- Some depressed people experience a significant weight loss or gain. "Significant" is generally considered to be a 5% weight loss or gain in a month when not trying.
- People suffering from MDE will generally have minimal problems going to sleep only to wake up in the early morning hours and have trouble getting back to sleep. A less common experience is sleeping more than the person's usual pattern.
- Some persons with MDE become agitated and others slow down. Some people become agitated mentally and physically. For example, if an officer were to interview patrons after a barroom brawl, they might report that it was obvious that the subject was looking for a fight the moment he walked through the door. If the officer were to ask the subject what was going on with him, he might say he just broke up with his girlfriend. Other people slow down mentally and physically.
- People with MDE often feel exhausted or lack energy. Decreased energy, tiredness, and weariness are common even without physical exertion. Even the smallest tasks seem to require substantial effort.
- The subject's family members may be on scene and report that he was really bad last week but they all thought he was getting better. In fact, this observation may be accurate. Last week, he did not have enough energy to put a suicide plan together. This week, he is better and has the energy to act.
- Subjects may feel worthless and guilty even about circumstances over which they have no control. It is for this reason that negotiators should be extremely careful about introducing non-law enforcement persons into an incident. The subject may feel guilty about things he has done or feel he has let these very people down. As negotiators, we do not want to heighten these feelings, but make the negotiation seem very private between the negotiator and subject.

- Diminished ability to think, concentrate, or make decisions. If the subject has decreased energy there will not be the usual conversational pace. The subject will be talking slowly, take a long time to answer, and sometimes the answer will not fit the negotiator's question.
- Recurrent thoughts of death or suicide are common.

Treatment

Treatment is highly successful, with 85% of institutionalized patients being discharged in a matter of two or three months.

Communication Suggestions

- If psychomotor retardation is present, you may have to wait longer than usual for a reply.
- Friends and relatives may provoke or escalate feelings of worthlessness and guilt.
- Beware of sudden improvements that are unrelated to your negotiation. Sudden, unexplained improvements, even reassurances to the negotiator, may indicate that the subject has made up his mind to proceed with the suicide. The decision to actually commit suicide has been made and he is now more at peace.
- Keep your time perspective in the here and now. The negotiator should offer a promise of immediate help not assurances that the subject will be feeling better in the months to come.
- The subject will generally require a small body space. A negotiator approached a depressed subject who was seated on a park bench. The man had a knife to a child's throat. The negotiator seated himself next to the man, patted him on the shoulder and assured him that help was available. This negotiation approach is not being advocated here but illustrates how close the negotiator managed to get to the subject. It would be difficult to do the same thing with paranoid or agitated symptoms.
- A depressed subject will generally be honest and straightforward with the negotiator.

- The negotiator should beware of "suicide by cop." Though exact numbers are not available, suicidal persons have killed and attempted to kill officers acting in the role of negotiator in an effort to provoke the police into killing them.
- Discuss real-world vs. abstract concepts when working with depressed persons. Negotiators should avoid discussing abstract concepts such as theology because it is a potential verbal and emotional minefield. Negotiators should ask, "Are you cold, hungry, thirsty, etc.?" and suggest going somewhere more comfortable to talk about the subject's problem.
- Negotiators should attempt to postpone the suicidal action as opposed to changing the subject's mood. It is acceptable to offer immediate assistance and tell the subject that, if that help fails, suicide is still an option at a later time. The negotiator can point out that officers cannot always be there to stop them. It is unlikely that a negotiator will make the suicidal person happy but the negotiator may be able to get him past the suicidal impulse.
- Active listening skills should be used to build empathy and establish a rapport with the subject. Without the development of such rapport, the negotiator may never even learn that the subject is suicidal.

APPENDIX A

Appendix A

SUICIDE INTERVENTION FLOW CHART

USE ACTIVE LISTENING WITH PERSONS IN CRISIS
- Emotion-label
- Reflect/mirror
- Paraphrase
- Open-ended questions
- Use silence
- Minimal encouragers
- "I" messages

↓

CLUES TO SUICIDAL INTENT
- Hopelessness/helplessness
- Flat mood
- Appears and sounds depressed
- Has expressed suicidal intent

↓

IF THERE IS *ANY* POSSIBILITY OF SUICIDE

ASK:

"Are you going to commit suicide?"

↓

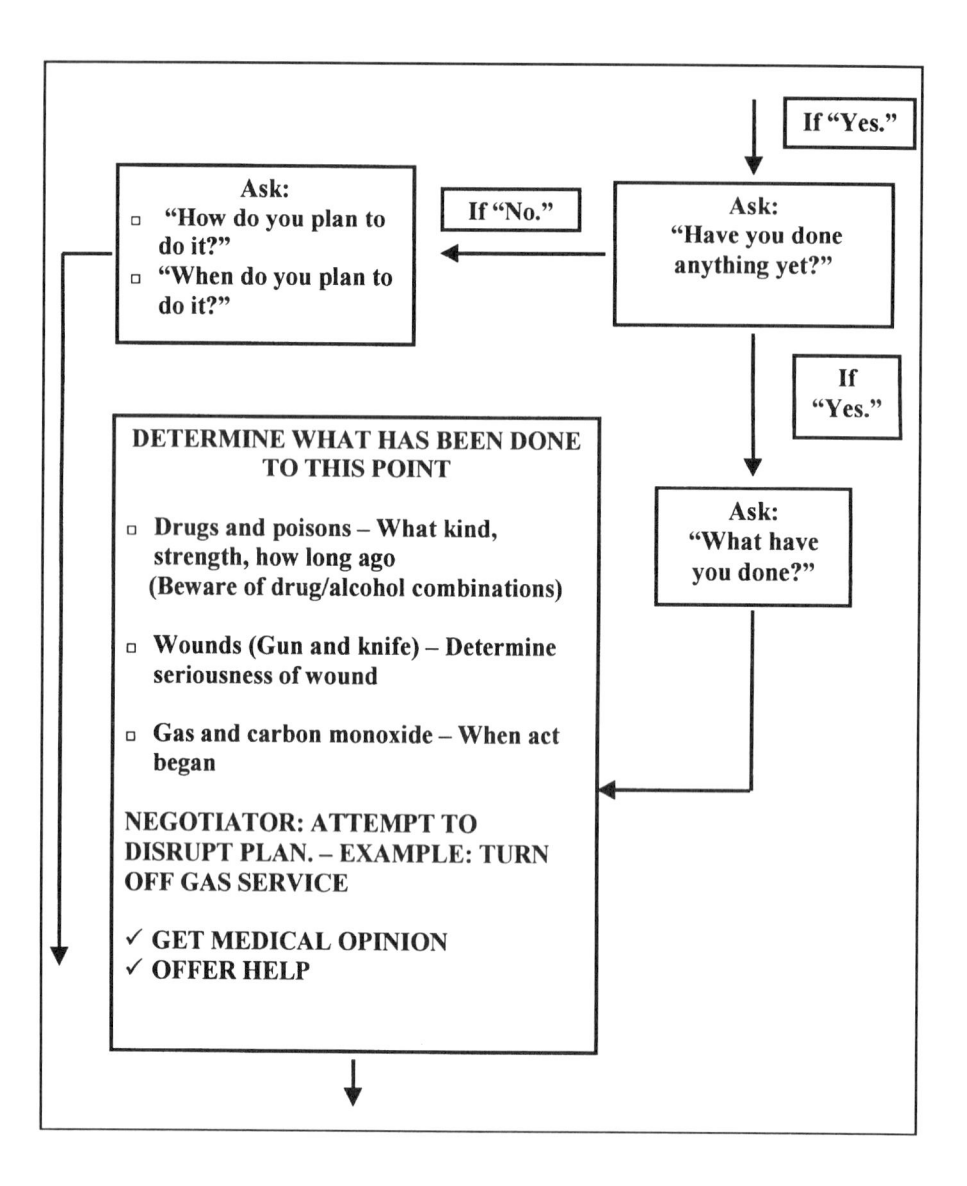

```
                                                      If "Yes."
                                                         ↓
      Ask:                              Ask:
  □ "How do you plan to    If "No."    "Have you done
    do it?"               ←──────────   anything yet?"
  □ "When do you plan to
    do it?"
                                                         │
                                                      If "Yes."
                                                         ↓
     DETERMINE WHAT HAS BEEN DONE
              TO THIS POINT                  Ask:
                                          "What have
   □ Drugs and poisons – What kind,        you done?"
     strength, how long ago
     (Beware of drug/alcohol combinations)

   □ Wounds (Gun and knife) – Determine
     seriousness of wound

   □ Gas and carbon monoxide – When act
     began

   NEGOTIATOR: ATTEMPT TO
   DISRUPT PLAN. – EXAMPLE: TURN
   OFF GAS SERVICE

   ✓ GET MEDICAL OPINION
   ✓ OFFER HELP
                    ↓
```

REDUCE OR REMOVE LETHALITY

- Drugs and poisons – Get the subject to vomit, walk and stay awake
- Wounds – Put weapon down or away, stop bleeding
- Gas – Turn off gas or car, open door or window

ANY CONCESSION *MAY* BE PROGRESS

DETERMINE WHAT PRECIPITATED THE PROBLEM

Ask:
"What has happened in the last day or two to make you want to kill yourself?"

GET SUBJECT TO TALK AND VENTILATE EMOTIONS

- Identify the "hook" and use it
- Identify and talk about any recent loss
- Identify the objective of the suicide

If appropriate, ask:
"Do you want to *hurt/get even* with *whomever* or do you want to die?"

WORK WITH SUBJECT TO DEVELOP ALTERNATIVES TO SUICIDE

- List all possible alternatives, even the bad ones, and then determine the least objectionable alternative.

- Ask: "If you could somehow have things your way, how would they be?"

DEVELOP PLAN TO ACHIEVE THE MOST REALISTIC OPTION

- Be specific.
- Be realistic.

AT THE END OF THE INCIDENT

- Follow through with any plans or promises made.
- Contact the appropriate agency regarding the suicide threat.

APPENDIX B

Appendix B

Interview Guide for Investigators

Subject Background

Subject Number _____
Initial call:
Responding officer or deputy's name:
Source's name: **Source's age:**
Source's relationship to subject:
Interviewer's name:
Interviewer's assessment of source:
Person's (refer to subject by name) full name:

- Other names he has used:
- Name that person prefers:
- Do you have a current photograph of person? (Yes) ☐ (No) ☐
- How has he changed since this photograph was taken?
- Obtain current identification record
- Does the subject belong to a gang, and if so, what gang?
- Are there any pets in the residence, and if so, what pets?
- Does today's date have any special significance for the subject such as the anniversary of a family event? If so, what is the significance of today's date?

Descriptive information
Date of birth: Age: Race:
Height: Weight: Hair color: Eye color:
Can you describe what he is wearing? (Yes) ☐ (No) ☐
If yes, describe his clothes.

Educational level
Did not complete high school ☐
Completed high school ☐
Completed college ☐ What was his major?
Completed graduate school ☐ What was his major?

Weapons information
What kind of weapon(s) does person have with him?
How do you know?
Has person ever used a weapon against anyone? Yes ☐ No ☐
If yes, describe the incident:
Has person ever been in the military? Yes ☐ No ☐
If yes, describe his military experience:
Has person ever received any kind of weapons training? Yes ☐ No ☐
If yes, tell me about the weapons training.

Similar incidents
Has he ever done anything like this incident before? Yes ☐ No ☐
If yes, describe that incident to me.
What was the outcome of the previous incident?
Where and when did that incident happen?

Indicators of impulsivity
Does person complain of people "getting in his face?" Yes ☐ No ☐
How often does he get into physical fights?
How often does he get into verbal fights?
Has person ever been arrested for assault? Yes ☐ No ☐
If yes, how many times?
Number of outstanding parking tickets:
Number of speeding tickets:
Other indicators of impulsivity:

Drug/alcohol history
Preferred drug/drink:
Do you believe person to be under the influence now?

When was the last time he used this drug or alcohol?
How long has person been using drugs and/or alcohol?
What is his usual behavior while under the influence?
What is his usual behavior while in withdrawal?
Is he a member of any 12-step program such as Alcoholics Anonymous or Narcotics Anonymous, and if so, what are his sponsor's name and telephone number?

Suicide
Has he said anything about committing suicide? Yes ☐ No ☐
If yes, what was said?
Has he ever attempted suicide? Yes ☐ No ☐
When was the last time he attempted suicide?
Describe each prior attempt:
Has anyone in the family attempted or committed suicide? Yes ☐ No ☐
Who in the family has attempted or committed suicide?
Has he seen a doctor recently? Yes ☐ No ☐
What was the doctor's name?
What was his complaint to the doctor?
What can you tell me about that doctor visit(s)?
If he was diagnosed, what was the diagnosis?
If any medication was prescribed, what was it?
Has person been taking the medication as prescribed?
How has he been feeling recently?
Has person been having sleeping problems? Yes ☐ No ☐
If yes, describe them:
Has person lost or gained weight without trying recently? Yes ☐ No ☐
Has person been giving away personal possessions? Yes ☐ No ☐

Mental-health history
Has he ever seen a mental-health professional? Yes ☐ No ☐
What was that doctor's name?
What brought about that visit(s)?
What can you tell me about that visit(s)?
If he was diagnosed, what was the diagnosis?
If any medication prescribed, what was it?
Has person been taking the medication as prescribed?
How has he been feeling recently?

Relationship to victim (**No prior relationship** ☐)
Give me a history of the relationship between person and (victim's name).

What has been happening in their relationship recently?
Has he injured (victim's name) in the past? Yes ☐ No ☐
Do the injuries appear to be increasingly frequent and/or severe? Yes ☐ No ☐

Current stressors
What has happened to bring on this incident?
What other stressors has he been experiencing recently?

Coping with stress
How does he normally cope with stress?
What has he been doing recently to cope with stress?
Has he been doing things recently that are not like him? If so, what has he been doing?

Interests
What does he enjoy doing in his spare time?
Has he been doing this activity recently?
What kind of books and magazines does he read?

Occupational history
What kinds of jobs has he held?
Does he do anything on his job or in his spare time that he feels he is particularly good at or is especially knowledgeable about?

Other
Is there anything else that you think we should know about (person) that we have not asked about?

Friends, relatives and others close to person

Name   Age
  Relationship

Name   Age
  Relationship

Name   Age
  Relationship

Name   Age
  Relationship

Name   Age
  Relationship

Name   Age
  Relationship

APPENDIX C

Appendix C
Overview of Active Listening Techniques

Emotion Labeling

You sound (emotion heard by negotiator).
You seem (emotion heard by negotiator).
I hear (emotion heard by negotiator).

Paraphrasing

Are you saying (what negotiator has heard in negotiator's words)?
Are you telling me (what negotiator has heard in negotiator's words)?

Reflecting or Mirroring

Repeat back the subject's last word or phrase as a question.
Example: Subject — "The way she acts just tears me up."
Negotiator — "Tears you up?"

Open-Ended Questions

> Questions that cannot be answered with a "yes" or "no." Open-ended questions often begin with who, what, when and where — but not why.

Minimal Encouragers

> Words or even sounds such as those made over the telephone to let the other party know that a person is listening.

Silence

> The negotiator should use silence just before and immediately after making an important point.

"I" Message

> I feel (the emotion the negotiator is feeling) when you (the subject's behavior) because (the negotiator's reason).

APPENDIX D

Appendix D

The Continuing Need for Training

Obvious lessons to come out of the tragic bombing in Oklahoma City are the constant need for vigilance against senseless acts of violence and the continuing need for training. No one and no place is safe from random acts of terror, whether committed by near-mythic Middle Eastern terrorists or heartland-of-America "good ol'boys" with a paranoid grievance against the federal government. Emergency personnel, who did a superb job, reported to the media that they had conducted drills and other practice sessions before the bombing. When tragedy strikes, nothing surpasses quality training in coping with the event.

"What kind of person could commit an act like the Oklahoma City bombing?" is a question often asked by the media in the aftermath. For those of us who have been in law enforcement for a while the answer is tragically simple; too many. Already mentioned are a couple of types, the terrorist or paranoid person with a grievance. Also envisioned as possibilities are paranoid schizophrenics on a mission, psychopaths with a score to settle, or any number of other possibilities. With as many people as there are in the United States, it requires a frighteningly small percentage of them to concoct a murderous scenario such as seen in Oklahoma City.

In the media, too, are questions involving prevention. Here is another question, "What crime have we ever been able to prevent?"

Some crimes seem to go out of "style" as opposed to being prevented. If we cannot prevent a crime or crimes, what can we do? The answer; prepare. Preparation involves training.

Yesterday's "hostage negotiators" have become today's "crisis negotiators" because negotiators have been responding to such a wide variety of incidents. Today, negotiators respond to any kind of incident where the boss needs an officer to talk to a bad guy. In talking to negotiators from around the world, one is struck with the diversity of negotiator call outs. Commanders expect negotiators to be prepared to talk to anyone under any conditions. Suppose a patrol officer or a security officer at the Federal Building in Oklahoma City had stopped the vehicle loaded with explosives. Who in Oklahoma City would have been called to negotiate the incident to a non-violent conclusion? Law enforcement negotiators.

Negotiation skills are just as perishable as tactical skills. We must have continual training and practice to meet the threat to human lives from constantly changing sources. None of us can predict the madness the human mind is capable of instigating. We can conceive of horribly tragic bombings or nerve gas attacks but not many of us have gone so far as to plan a response or to train for their occurrence. The FBI trained for such "unlikely" scenarios as a cruise ship being hijacked and for multiple, simultaneous hostage takings. Then came the Achille Lauro hijacking and the Atlanta/Oakdale prison sieges.

Emergency medical personnel in Oklahoma City undoubtedly grumbled and groaned through every training day. "A mass medical emergency here in Oklahoma City? It just won't happen here. New York or Chicago, maybe, but not here."

It probably will not happen in your town or city either.

Probably.

APPENDIX E

Appendix E
The Dangers of Manipulating Anxiety Levels

Shortly after the inception of modern hostage negotiation techniques in the 1970s, manipulation of anxiety techniques were being taught and used by many law enforcement agencies. Originally, this technique was intended for use when it was felt that the subject was getting too comfortable and even enjoying the attention he was receiving as a result of the hostage-taking incident. The procedure was to raise the subject's anxiety level, then lower it, then raise it again, and so on. The idea being that raising and lowering the subject's anxiety or arousal level would wear him out faster and thereby bring the incident to resolution faster.

Later, some agencies started using the technique to pressure subjects into talking to the negotiator. In fact, employing the technique to get people to talk became its primary and only use with many agencies. Curiously though, these same departments often will say they do not employ manipulation of anxiety techniques.

In the 1980s, the FBI began to see some dangers involved in the technique's original intent. The FBI has never endorsed or taught manipulation of anxiety as a means of prodding a subject into talking. There is a vast difference between someone who is calmly sitting out a hostage situation and enjoying the attention he is receiving and someone who is too frightened or mistrustful of the authorities to speak. From the outside, however, the two situations may look alike.

There is relatively little danger to anyone in situations where the subject is too calm but the reverse is certainly not true. While it is easy to "jack" someone up, to put a cap on his fear and anxiety is extremely difficult. Once negotiators start the process of raising his anxiety, how can they be sure that they can stop its rise before he does something dangerous?

Some police departments will do things like throw pebbles up on the roof or against the window of a residence or do other things to scare the subject. If sufficiently scared, subjects frequently do begin talking to or, more commonly, screaming at the negotiator. The most seductive aspect of this technique, though dangerous, is the fact that it often works. During the incident at Ruby Ridge, ID, for example, the negotiator's first contact and several subsequent contacts were initiated by the subject after he was unintentionally frightened.

The FBI strongly suspected that this technique might be dangerous with some personality types, especially paranoid schizophrenics. During a hostage negotiation seminar, it was suggested to a group of police officers that, if applied inappropriately, the technique might panic certain subjects into a suicide, a homicide-suicide, a suicide-by-cop, or attack on the police. A police officer said that his department had thrown some pebbles up on a roof to get a paranoid schizophrenic to talk. He said the subject panicked and charged out of the house with a shotgun leveled at officers on the perimeter. The subject was killed. The FBI and others have long taught its negotiators to avoid tricks and lies for a variety of reasons. Manipulation of anxiety is one of those tricks that should be avoided.

Though especially dangerous with paranoid persons, the danger of this technique's backfiring is too great to be employed against anyone. With subjects who are too frightened, paranoid, or mistrustful of us to speak, we will confirm their beliefs and suspicions about the world outside by deliberately raising their anxiety level. In this common situation, the subject is already so frightened and terrified of us that he is refusing to talk. To suggest that adding to his fear may be helpful is foolhardy and extremely dangerous.

Negotiators spend much of their time trying to calm frightened people, which often is not easy. Raising anxiety levels, on the other hand, is very easy and has actually been entertaining for some bored persons on the inner perimeter. There have been situations where people on the perimeter were deliberately scaring the bad guy for no appropriate reason and without the knowledge of negotiators or command.

Another problem with the technique is the probability that the subject will connect the negotiator with what is going on. The establishment of negotiator–subject rapport has been essential and is often the essential factor in the successful resolution of many negotiated incidents. Negotiators should be trying to build rapport with the bad guy, and if he suspects that the negotiator is also participating in harassment tactics, that activity will undermine the negotiator's rapport-building efforts.

Frightening the subject may even make the situation more dangerous for the tactical team. Tactical teams rehearse entries before an entry is made. They will find an identical room or building, or line one out in the dirt or on a gymnasium floor. They will choreograph their moves so each member of the team fully understands where he or she will be going and where their firing lanes will be.

A fact that is unappreciated by many tactical and negotiation teams is that every time the subject is frightened, we induce him to rehearse. Every time the subject is frightened, he moves into a defensive position and thinks about how he will respond to the threat of a tactical team's entry. Tactical teams rely on speed, violence of action, and surprise. One of the reasons explosive breaching is such a potentially valuable technique is because it is fast, violent, and a surprise. The subject has not rehearsed for the scenario of the tactical team explosively coming through a wall.

As with many things done in negotiation, negotiators can find examples of situations where a specific technique was attempted and worked. Negotiators can also find instances where the same technique lead to disaster. In some ways, using manipulation of anxiety techniques is analogous to using third-party intermediaries. There is no question that sometimes using TPIs works, but sometimes people die. The question for negotiators and command: "Is this one of those instances where this technique will lead to success or will it lead to disaster?"

APPENDIX F

Appendix F
The Negotiation Effort

The negotiation effort is far more than a team of negotiators talking to a "bad guy" over the telephone. What negotiators are saying to the subject is only part of the message being conveyed to him. In a sense, every crisis management component is part of the negotiation effort. When viewing negotiation in this manner, the negotiation effort not only includes what the negotiators say to the subject but also encompasses every observed move the tactical team makes, every radio and television broadcast the subject hears, and every decision made by management. For the negotiation effort to be maximally effective, all actions taken or not taken by each of the crisis components must communicate the same message. It is essential that all crisis management components follow the same strategy.

The crisis management components should meet early in the incident and regularly after that. Management must decide what message it wants to convey and how it should be conveyed. If management decides it wants to be tough, everybody is tough. Negotiators take a hard line. Tactical teams display an obvious presence. Management adopts a strong position that is reflected in its decisions and media releases. If management decides it wants to take a softer line, negotiators are more empathic. Tactical teams maintain a low profile and management is more conciliatory in its decision making. Management must make the decision on strategy and each component communicates management's message to the subject.

Periodically throughout the incident, the components must meet to discuss progress, evaluate their strategy, and make adjustments as necessary. If the crisis management team shifts its strategy, everyone on the component teams must be informed as to the impending change in strategy, what the new strategy is, and how the change will be implemented.

Expressing the same message to the subject obviously requires communication and agreement between crisis management components. If the components are not talking to each other and information is not passed down within their respective teams, it is unlikely that a single message will be communicated to the subject. What is required is not only interteam communication but intrateam communication. The actions of a single individual, if not in line with the current strategy, can destroy the efficacy of the negotiation effort and, perhaps, any chance of a peaceful resolution.

Management giving negotiators full rein or allowing them to "do their thing" does little good unless the entire management team and the tactical team know what the negotiators are doing and support them by sending the same message to the subject. Differing messages from each component leads to distrust of the negotiators, a belief by the subject that the negotiators have no influence with management, and a protracted incident or worse.

It is extremely difficult, if not impossible, for the negotiators to convince the subject that the authorities intend him no harm when tactical teams are, in full view of the subject, moving into position. Any movement by the tactical team while operating under this strategy must be accomplished with complete discretion. If negotiators are attempting to be reassuring, all components must act in accordance with that posture if management expects its negotiators to have credibility with the subject.

Every critical incident is unique and requires a game plan of its own just as each ballgame is unique and requires a game plan of its own. Some subjects can be persuaded and coaxed while others must be pressured to do the right thing.

One sure way to put pressure on a subject is to deliberately inject uncertainty into the equation. An easy means of instilling uncertainty in an adversary's mind is to convey multiple messages. His fear and paranoia will do the rest.

In a sense, every message communicated to the opposing side is part of the negotiation effort. Every person who conveys that message to the subject becomes part of the negotiation effort. Negotiators have tactical responsibilities such as the passing of intelligence information. Similarly, tactical-team members have negotiation responsibilities in the message they convey to the subject. It is not enough to know and respect the role of the other crisis management components. It is essential that all components view themselves as part of a single, unified effort and convey only one message to the subject if the desired outcome is to be achieved.

APPENDIX G

Appendix G

The Troubled State of Crisis Management

Over the last 25 years, crisis negotiators have developed and put into practice a set of guidelines that have proven to be remarkably successful. Tactical personnel have developed their techniques over a similar time span. Where are comparable crisis-management guidelines and techniques?

Crisis negotiators often say their priorities are the preservation of life, the apprehension of the subject, and the recovery and protection of property—but negotiators do not set departmental priorities, managers do. Most negotiators assume that their top management has the same priorities as the negotiation team, but do they? Have crisis managers discussed priorities in a management seminar? How much is management willing to pay in overtime? How much is management willing to inconvenience a city? What is management willing to expend in manpower? How far has management gone to develop mutual-aid pacts for that big incident that might occur at any time? When was the last time your chief or sheriff trained with your team?

Often in crisis management seminars we hear topics discussed such as the importance of intelligence flow, setting up a command post, keeping the noise level to a minimum, etc. There is an underlying assumption that good intelligence flow and crisis management structure will lead to good decision making. Unfortunately, this assumption is not always true. Sometimes, bad decisions are made despite the presence of good information and crisis management structure. Our top law enforcement managers need training and experience just as much as good negotiators and tactical personnel.

In many departments, the chief or sheriff delegates on-scene crisis management authority down to the sergeant or lieutenant level. In these departments, for the "routine" barricaded subject and other lower-profile situations, this arrangement works well. Is the chief or sheriff going to do the same thing when a high-profile situation comes along and the head of the state police and the FBI's Special Agent in Charge are on-scene and the state governor is calling for a report on negotiation progress? In our biggest incidents we have our most inexperienced managers, i.e., top management, attempting to direct the incident—and, incidentally, getting themselves killed in the process.

A number of years ago, the author reviewed 10 years of hostage, barricade, and suicide situations out of the FBI's annual report on law enforcement officers who had been killed the previous year. Almost half of the persons killed while attempting to negotiate were chiefs and sheriffs of smaller towns, cities, and counties. (Incidentally, almost all the negotiators in that study were killed while attempting to negotiate with suicidal persons.) Unfortunately, these individuals did not appear to have any training and many had only a few years in law enforcement. The incidents in which these law enforcement executives were killed were major ones for their areas and they apparently felt compelled to take personal command.

A few years ago, the Special Operations and Research Unit, now the Crisis Negotiation Unit, at the FBI Academy at Quantico, VA established a one-day course entitled "Hostage Negotiation and Tactics for Commanders." This course was established after receiving complaints from law enforcement officers from all over the U.S. about the lack of crisis management training and the reluctance of ranking officers to participate in training when it was available. The idea behind this one-day seminar was that managers would be provided an overview of negotiation and tactics and thereby know what their people were doing in a crisis situation. The course was restricted to one day because of the difficulty in getting law enforcement executives away from their desks and other responsibilities for more than a day at a time.

Despite good critiques, the course was dropped in a short period of time. Rather than potential on-scene commanders attending the course, negotiators and tactical people were attending. Students often commented that the course content was just what commanders needed to hear but the people who needed the training the most could not be lured into the classroom.

After a shooting by law enforcement, the persons investigating the shooting immediately put the officers on administrative leave and the officers' records, particularly their firearms training records, are pulled and scrutinized. The investigators look at their shooting scores, the weapons that they have qualified with, what courses they have fired, etc.

Someday, after a crisis situation has turned sour, some plaintiff's smart attorney is going to file suit against a law enforcement agency and subpoena the on-scene commander's training record. That opposing attorney is going to put the on-scene commander on the witness stand and ask, "What crisis management courses have you attended? What were you taught? Do you have your notes? Where can I get a copy of the lesson plan? Did you do any role-playing? What kinds of situations were depicted? What score did you achieve? Chief (Sheriff, Lieutenant, Captain, or Major), since merely passing a promotional exam or getting elected does not make you a crisis manager, what makes you think you are qualified to manage a situation where lives were held in the balance?" It could be a very embarrassing and expensive series of questions for some department or agency.

Crisis management needs enthusiasts. Crisis management needs people who are interested in crisis management as a discipline and not only participate in training but seek training and develop new crisis management ideas.

There are negotiation and tactical newsletters and journals and statewide or regional organizations. Is there anything comparable for crisis managers? Unfortunately, since the presentation of these ideas will appear in a negotiators' reference book perhaps all the writer has achieved is some "venting."

APPENDIX H

Appendix H

A Negotiator's View of the Incident at Ruby Ridge

Crisis negotiation, in some respects, is an inherently nasty business in that we negotiators often find ourselves bargaining for lives and, occasionally, people die. At other times, it is enormously rewarding and because of those good times I have been involved in crisis negotiation for more than 20 years. This account is not the story of one of those good times.

I would like to tell you more than a lengthy war story. I will tell you the negotiation team's reasoning, where we could have done better and where we did well. One of the very unfortunate things about the incident at Ruby Ridge and, a few months later, Waco, was that many things—including negotiations—were done very, very well. Those accomplishments will be forever overshadowed by the outcomes of those incidents and there is a lesson to be learned right there.

There have been many investigations, allegations, and developments since the conclusion of the Ruby Ridge incident and I will not go into those developments, as they have been torturously investigated and documented elsewhere. My point here is to simply tell the story from a law enforcement negotiator's perspective based on what the negotiation team knew at the time of the incident.

To this writing, I have not read extensive accounts of this incident or watched the Senate hearings, though I did testify. Until recently,

I considered myself a potential witness and I did not want to pollute my recollections of the event with the opinions, speculation, and observations of others. As a result, some readers may be more informed about the non-negotiation aspects of this situation than I. What I do know is what my negotiation team and I did.

From the very beginning I had a bad feeling about this incident. My only prior knowledge of the Weaver family was from a national newsmagazine that I had casually read aboard an airplane some weeks earlier. With only this knowledge, I told my wife, Donna, before I left, "I really don't want to do this one."

The Initial Crime

In October 1989, the Bureau of Alcohol, Tobacco and Firearms (ATF) bought two sawed-off shotguns from Randall Weaver. Weaver contended that he was set up by ATF because he did not cooperate in their hope to have him act as an informant. In December 1990, Weaver was indicted on the charge of manufacturing the illegal shotguns. In January 1991, ATF and the local sheriff arrested Weaver. At the time of his arrest, Weaver's pregnant wife, Vicki, was with him. Weaver alleges that she was thrown to the ground and otherwise mistreated. In February 1991, Weaver failed to appear at a hearing and a bench warrant was issued for his arrest.

Weaver sought refuge on his mountaintop, where he garnered a considerable amount of local public sympathy. He remained on the mountain for about 18 months. There was no information that he ever went into town.

I was told that Weaver was kicked out of the Aryan Nation for being too radical in that he wanted to train Aryan Nation children in firearms as he had trained his own children. It was believed that he trained his entire family in the use of weapons and family members were known in the community as being good with those weapons. He drilled his family in taking up firing positions on signal if the government came after him. I was also advised that Weaver let it be known that he would kill any law enforcement person who came after him.

The Weaver family consisted of Randall Weaver, age 44 at the time, wife Vicki, 42, daughter Sara, 16, son Samuel, 14, Rachel, 10, and Elisheba (I was told that her name was Elizabeth), 8 months.

Kevin Harris, a young man who appeared to be in his 20s, spent a lot of time at the Weavers' cabin. I was told that Randall treated him like a son.

Friday, 8/21/92

Meanwhile, the United States Marshal Service (USMS) was attempting to determine a means whereby they could safely arrest Weaver by making scouting trips on the mountain top where Weaver built his home, Ruby Ridge. Again, what I am about to relate are the facts as I understood them to be at the outset of the incident. I understand and the reader should be aware there are now other versions of this story.

On the morning of 8/21/92, the USMS sent two scouting teams up Weaver's mountain. They had orders to avoid a confrontation with the Weaver family but a dog belonging to the Weavers spotted one team of marshals.

One of the persons on this team was William F. "Bill" Degan, 42, who was married and the father of two. Degan and his team fled down the mountain with the Weaver family dog, Samuel Weaver, and Kevin Harris in pursuit. The dog was gaining on Degan so he turned and fired at the animal, killing it. Degan then stepped off the dirt road and as Samuel and Kevin passed him, Degan announced his presence. I was told that Kevin Harris turned, fired, and hit Degan in the chest.

Randall Weaver fired rounds from his shotgun and 9mm handgun as a signal to retreat to the house. As Samuel and Kevin were returning back up the mountain, Degan apparently returned fire, hit Samuel, then subsequently died from his wounds about 10 minutes later. The remaining marshals stayed on the mountain, believing themselves to be pinned down.

At approximately 5:30 p.m., I was notified by telephone that Hostage Rescue Team (HRT) was probably going to Idaho and that I would be accompanying them. (I was in the Special Operations and Research Unit, now the Crisis Negotiation Unit, at the FBI Academy and was in no way a part of the HRT.) A short time later, I got the word from HRT that we were, in fact, being deployed. I went to the HRT's headquarters and was told to immediately proceed to Andrews Air Force Base. I was informed that the airplane would leave in one hour and I was about one hour from the air base. I viewed this news as a semi-legitimate reason to try out my new sports car and headed up Interstate 95 at 90 miles per hour. The plane left about four hours later. We departed Andrews Air Force Base aboard two United States Air Force C141s at 12:30 a.m. en route to Fairchild Air Force Base near Spokane.

Saturday, 8/22/92

Upon our arrival in Spokane, a caravan was formed and we drove to Bonners Ferry, in the upper part of the Idaho panhandle not far from the border with Canada. We arrived there at 7:22 a.m. and received a briefing from the HRT commander, Assistant Special Agent in Charge (ASAC) Richard "Dick" Rogers, who was part of an HRT advance team. We were told that the marshals were no longer pinned down and that the only USMS casualty was Bill Degan.

At the briefing, we were told the Rules of Engagement (ROE). The ROE authorized the HRT to fire upon any adult male with a weapon but they are not to fire into the house. We were also told that, "this will be no long siege." The HRT and I received additional details regarding the current situation from other members of the advance team. After the briefing we proceeded to the Command Post (CP) at the base of the mountain known as Ruby Ridge.

It was clear to me that there were to be no negotiations. I told ASAC Rogers that if there was not going to be any negotiation I would work with his intelligence-gathering component. He said, "Okay."

My misgivings about this incident began to grow from my initial "bad vibes." The first thing that troubled me was the ROE but I satisfied myself with the fact that the advance party had a sizeable jump on me in terms of gathering intelligence and maybe they were appropriate. Surely, I thought, the ROE were cleared with FBIHQ and the FBI's Legal Counsel Division.

In all fairness to ASAC Rogers, and despite my 20-year commitment to negotiation, every day tactical teams somewhere in the U.S. surround an objective, order the occupants out, the occupants comply and the incident is over. My hope was that this incident would conclude in that fashion.

Finally, in terms of rank and position, I was heavily outweighed by the commander of HRT, and the HRT's presence on scene is awesome. When these 50 vigorously selected, highly trained, physically fit, superbly equipped men arrive at an incident, it is very impressive. They have the best equipment money can buy. They bring with them a large command and control tent that "pops" up in minutes, computers and fax machines and, in this case, six vehicles including a helicopter.

I did not think we needed all that response. At the conclusion of the incident, I told FBI inspectors that the agency had overreacted and the incident could have been more appropriately managed by a couple of negotiators and a five-man tactical team. We had a man, though a "cop-killer," barricaded on the top of a mountain with his family. He was no danger to the public or further danger to us if we were careful. We were not blocking any downtown traffic or tying up a city somewhere. In some respects, it was a relatively "routine" bad situation, and should have been managed that way. Randall Weaver was considered in some quarters, perhaps in no small part due to his own rhetoric, a right-wing terrorist. The HRT is a highly trained, antiterrorist organization and if they are on scene, it must be bad.

The command post (CP) was several miles from protesters and a roadblock down a one-lane dirt road. Along this dirt road was a small bridge that I understand that the FBI rebuilt to accommodate some of the heavier equipment that later arrived. Initially, there were just a few military-style tents but the number of tents rapidly grew, as did the number of people on-scene. A one point a local oldtimer said to me, "You know, son, if we get just a few more men out here, we can get our own zip code."

Early Saturday afternoon, FBI Special Agent in Charge (SAC) Gene Glenn, the on-scene commander, said that he wanted me to be the primary negotiator. I was told to write a crisis negotiation section for the operations plan. The previous plan was rejected by FBIHQ because it did not include negotiations. With the suggestions of SAC Glenn, ASAC Rogers, and USMS personnel, I wrote the following:

"A negotiator will go forward to the residence in the armored personnel carrier (APC). When the APC is in view of the house it will stop and the negotiator will make the following statement:

Mr. Weaver, this is Fred Lanceley of the FBI. You should understand that we have warrants for the arrest of yourself and Mr. Harris. I would like you to accept a telephone so that we can talk and work out how you will come out of the house without further violence. I would like you or one of your children to come out of the house, unarmed, pick up the telephone and return to the house.

At the conclusion of this statement, the APC will proceed forward, drop the telephone, and withdraw. If Weaver or a child retrieves the telephone, the negotiator will attempt to initiate a dialogue."

> *Negotiators' comment: I did not know it at the time, but at 6:01 p.m., an HRT sniper fired two shots. I debriefed the sniper later that evening when he came down the mountain. He told me that on the first shot, he fired just as Randall Weaver was turning the corner of the "birthing shed." (I was told that when Vicki or Sara Weaver had their periods, they stayed in the birthing shed separate from the men in Old Testament fashion. Additionally, Vicki Weaver had given birth to Elizabeth in the "birthing shed." Hence, its name.) The sniper said that Weaver swung himself around the corner just as he fired and caused him to miss the shot. He said that he knew he missed the shot because he saw splinters fly off the corner of the shed.*
>
> *The sniper then aimed his rifle at the door and fired a second round. He said he saw Kevin Harris go down with a possible hit to the shoulder. He added that Harris might also have tripped going over the doorsill or he might have just been "hitting the dirt" as he did in the shootout with the marshals.*
>
> *What actually happened was that his first round went through Randall Weaver's fleshy upper arm and out his armpit before it hit the corner of the "birthing shed." His second round did hit Kevin Harris in the shoulder and then into his chest but not before inflicting a fatal wound to Vicki Weaver's head. The Weaver baby, Elisheba, was in her arms as she was attempting to open the door wider for Randall Weaver and Kevin Harris.*
>
> *I believe the sniper's account of what had transpired was an accurate one, that is, to the best of his knowledge. I believe that he thought he missed Randall Weaver. I do not think that he saw Vicki Weaver and the baby inside the darkened doorway from a distance of at least 200 yards, and perhaps as much as 250 yards. The truly remarkable fact was that he missed what he was shooting at.*

Approximately 6:30 p.m.

I went up the mountain with several members of the HRT in an APC to drop off a portable telephone designed for crisis negotiators. We all sat in the APC with double layers of body armor, ballistic helmets and weapons drawn. No one spoke in the semidarkness as the tracked APC loudly rumbled and clawed its way up the steep dirt logging road. There was serious concern that the road and gate were mined or booby-trapped.

As we proceeded up the mountain in the APC, I began to wonder about the result of an accidental discharge in this tracked, steel box that I was riding in. A round would not stop ricocheting until one of us stopped it. With that realization and the thought that there was no way I could defend myself against an armor-piercing round in any case, I holstered my weapon. We encountered no mines or booby traps.

At the top of the mountain, the APC came to a stop and the crew door at the back was opened. When the door swung open I knew exactly where I was because I had spent the afternoon studying surveillance photographs of the residence and its surroundings. I immediately recognized two unmistakable bright blue barrels perched off the ground on a kind of scaffolding near the cabin.

I was also somewhat alarmed because we were so close to the house. We were no more than 20 yards away and I considered our position to be a provocative one. I understood Weaver to have armor-piercing rounds and I fully expected to hear rounds pinging off of, not through, the sides of the APC at any moment. Despite our seeming provocation, nothing happened.

At this point, I began thinking that Randall Weaver, despite his rhetoric, the shooting of Bill Degan, and his background with the Aryan Nation, was not as fanatical and dangerous as was generally believed. There were no booby traps on the gate, no mines in the road and he did not fire at the APC.

I read the announcement as written in the operations plan. I knew there had been a shooting and that was a bad enough position for a negotiator. What actually happened was even worse. I was in the unknowing, ridiculous, tragic position of asking Weaver to step out onto the front porch within an hour or so of his wife's being killed, Harris's being shot and Weaver's being wounded. I did not even know that Samuel Weaver had been killed on Friday in the shootout with the marshals.

After reading the announcement and dropping the telephone, we started making our way down the mountain. As Weaver had neither electricity nor telephone we laid down about one and a half miles of telephone wire.

The Government's Perspective

Both sides of this confrontation, the government and Weaver, had dug a very deep hole from which the negotiation team was to work. On the one hand, the government was convinced that Randall Weaver was a very dangerous individual. That conviction grew out of intelligence reports relating to his activity with the Aryan Nation and his being asked to leave because he was too radical. He was also known to keep weapons in the house and the whole family, including 10-year old Rachel, were trained in the use of weapons. As previously mentioned, before our trip up the mountain in the APC, it was thought that the road might be mined and the gate booby-trapped. Weaver was thought to possess armor-piercing ammunition and some of his neighbors were frightened of him and his family.

I was advised that Randall Weaver had told people that he would kill any law enforcement officer who came after him. As evidence that he was a man of his word, we had the body of Bill Degan.

At one point in the siege, I told an Assistant United States Attorney (AUSA) that to get Randall Weaver out of the house was going to take something creative. Maybe something legally creative. I suggested, as an example of legal creativity, that if convicted, he could do his time on the mountaintop. The AUSA said words to the effect that no judge would ever go along with that because Weaver might kill a passing hunter. He added his belief that we were never going to get him to come out anyway. He then turned and walked away from me. I was livid with rage.

> *Negotiator's comment: Any barricaded subject has a very limited number of options.*
>
> *1. He can commit suicide.*
> *2. He can commit homicide then suicide.*
> *3. He can surrender.*

> *If Weaver was not going to commit suicide or homicide, he has no other option but to surrender if we just have the patience to wait. He has to come out, eventually.*

As a further example of how dangerous Randall Weaver was thought to be, there was no 24-hour perimeter around the Weaver residence house but there was a tactical team perimeter around our command post area at the base of the mountain to protect us from him. I asked why we did not have a 24-hour perimeter around the residence and was informed that at the top of the mountain it is dark and wet, and the terrain is rocky. Someone might get hurt.

The HRT is equipped for just these conditions. I was incredulous and insulted for them especially since I consider them to be among the best-equipped, most highly trained, and select teams in the world. There was no 24-hour perimeter around the house until Sunday evening. At any point during Friday and Sunday nights, Weaver and his family could have walked away from the house and across the mountains.

Randall Weaver's Perspective

I have never spoken to Randall Weaver except during the siege but he had to have been thinking that all of his worst right-wing, nightmare beliefs had come true. Federal agents had killed his wife and son. He and Kevin had been shot. Armed federal agents surrounded him and helicopters were flying low over his house. He and his family were very frightened. Is it any wonder that he said nothing to me for days?

> *Negotiator's comment: All times are from the negotiators' log and all of the statements in quotes are just as they were read to the Weaver family. Though we had sophisticated, classified equipment on scene, I could not get a good-quality tape recorder though we did have a small pocket recorder. Feeling certain that the Weaver family would sue the FBI at the conclusion of the siege, I told negotiators to be sure to document everything that we said or did. We therefore scripted out our comments to Weaver and read them in our best conversational tones.*

9:45 p.m.

A Drug Abuse Resistance and Education (DARE) van was established as a base for negotiators. In the DARE van, our telephone to the Weavers was up and operating. We attempted to contact Weaver at 9:45 p.m., 10:00 p.m., 10:30 p.m., 11:00 p.m., and 11:30 p.m. All attempts met with no response. Over the telephone's receiver, raindrops could be heard hitting the telephone.

Sunday, 8/23/92

8:25 a.m.

Muffled voices, footsteps, and a barking, whining dog can be heard over the telephone. People are walking around in Weaver's yard but there is no perimeter to see what is going on. The telephone was rung with no answer.

8:28 a.m.

A small dog can be heard over the telephone.

8:30 a.m. and 8:45 a.m.

We attempted contact with no answer. The dog noises continue.

8:47 a.m. to 2:46 p.m.

Contacts were attempted approximately every 15 minutes with no response.

3:04 p.m.

The telephone wire was cut after having been run over by the APC.

Approximately 9:00 p.m.

I went to the top of the mountain to see what became the Forward Command Post.

> *Negotiator's comment: All negotiators' remarks were made to Weaver and his family over a remotely controlled vehicle commonly called a robot. The "robot" is a small, tracked machine that was originally developed for bomb technicians. It is equipped with a loudspeaker, a receiver, closed-circuit television camera and a shotgun. The shotgun is used by bomb technicians to blow up suspicious packages. During this incident, the shotgun was not loaded. I had Bo Gritz look at the shotgun so there would be no question later that it was unloaded. I do not believe though, that the Weavers saw the shotgun until the siege was almost over.*

> *Each time I called out to Weaver, I gave him time to get to a position in the house where he could hear me. My "threshold diagnosis" was that Weaver was not the kind of individual who would indulge in light chitchat or like it if I attempted to get too "chummy" with him. As a result, I tried to remain somewhat formal and give him something to think about every time I addressed him.*

10:01 p.m.

"Mr. Weaver, please go to a place in the house where you can hear me. I'll wait.

Mr. Weaver, this is Fred Lanceley. I am a negotiator with the FBI. I spoke to you briefly yesterday.

Mr. Weaver, we have moved a remote-controlled vehicle up to your house. This vehicle will allow you and I to talk. All you have to do is speak up and I should be able to hear you. I assure you that this vehicle is no threat to you or your family."

10:05 p.m. and 10:15 p.m.

"Mr. Weaver, this is Fred again.

We have found the body of a young man I presume to be Samuel. I urgently request that you provide some guidance as to how you want us to proceed with arrangements for Samuel. We do not want to take any steps that may violate your religious beliefs at this time of grief for your family.

Please communicate your wishes to us by speaking up."

> *Negotiator's comment: The body of Samuel "Sammy" Weaver was found in the birthing shed by a member of the HRT who was manning the inner perimeter. Finding Sammy's body was one of the most dramatic moments of the siege for me. I did not know that he had been killed on Friday and one of my initial fears was that Randall Weaver might kill his family and himself.*
>
> *The HRT member whispered into his radio that he had found the body of a young white male with a small-caliber bullet wound to his forehead. (What he actually saw in the darkness was a smudge on Sammy's forehead and a .22 caliber shell casing lying on the floor next to him. He apparently thought that a .22 caliber weapon had killed Sammy.) This was the first I had heard of Sammy's death*

and I remember thinking, "My God! He's killing his family!" I could not imagine that Weaver would not speak up and tell me how he wanted Sammy's body cared for and I attempted to use this topic to initiate some kind of dialogue.

10:30 p.m.

"Mr. Weaver, you must understand that we are not going to go away. We have to talk. Let's begin by making arrangements for Samuel. Give us the name of a friend you would like us to contact so they can take care of Samuel for you."

Negotiator's comment: Here, I violated one of my own suggestions to student negotiators. In the classroom, I advocate that when using the pronoun "we" it should mean the negotiator and subject and not "we," the authorities. I corrected this usage of "we" later on.

10:49 p.m.

"Mr. Weaver, for your information, the County Coroner has taken custody of Samuel's body. In a situation like this one, it is standard procedure to do an autopsy. I don't know how you feel about the performance of an autopsy but it will be done unless you tell us otherwise."

Negotiator's comment: Here, I was attempting to put Weaver in a double bind. He did not want to talk but I did not think he would want an autopsy done either. I thought that the idea of an autopsy would cause him to start talking to me. It did not work. He said nothing.

10:52 p.m.

To ensure that Weaver could actually hear me I asked that he move a curtain in the upstairs window to indicate that he could hear. He did not.

11:15 p.m.

"Mr. Weaver, I know it has been a very difficult three days for you, your family, friends, and supporters. The only way we can get all this behind us is to begin talking. Like I said before, we are not going to go away. I am sure you realize things could get worse. Is there any point to putting Mrs. Weaver, Rachel, Sara, and Elizabeth through a worsening situation? I've been told that Mr. Harris may need medical attention. Let's get that done. Talk to me."

> *Negotiator's comment: One of the things I tell negotiation students is to be certain of getting people's names correct. In the USMS briefing book, I read Elisheba's name to be Elizabeth. Unfortunately, I erroneously called her Elizabeth throughout the siege.*

11:52 p.m.
"Mr. Weaver, I have mentioned several topics tonight that I hope you, your family, and Mr. Harris will think about and talk over.

If you love your family like I love mine, I am sure you have some wishes for Samuel. Tell me about them. Provide a name for me to contact.

Tell me what I can do or say to get all this behind us. Help me to help you and your family, Mr. Weaver.

One more time, we are not going to go away. You and I can begin to end this nightmare for you, your wife and children.

Think about these things, Mr. Weaver. Talk about them with Mrs. Weaver and Mr. Harris. Let's you and I have a talk in the morning that will put an end to this situation."

Monday, 8/24/92

> *Negotiator's comment: Because of steep terrain, only tracked or four-wheel drive vehicles could make it up the mountain and they went up the mountain only periodically. Upon my arrival at the forward command post I was told that 20 to 30 minutes earlier, Weaver was demanding that the robot be moved.*

8:07 a.m.
"Mr. Weaver, this is Fred. Good morning. I just came back up the mountain.

I've been told that you were saying something about 45 minutes ago. I'm sorry I missed it. The people out here could not make out what you were saying at the time but I should be able to hear you now. What I have been told is that you may have some concerns

about the vehicle in front of your house. I want to hear what you have to say. Please talk to me Mr. Weaver."
8:10 a.m.

Weaver was told that the helicopter sounds he was probably hearing were a routine over-flight. There was no cause for alarm.
8:15 a.m.

I repeated the 8:07 a.m. statement.
8:42 a.m.

"Mr. Weaver, the guys on the perimeter have told me that you were concerned about the vehicle and that you sounded angry. If you don't talk to me, I can't help you. Allow me to help you."
10:32 a.m. and again at 10:34 a.m.

"Randall Weaver, we will be moving the vehicle forward because we're not sure we can hear you. Again, I want to assure you that this vehicle cannot harm you or your family in any way. This machine is pretty amazing but it may break down or we may roll it and we'll lose communication. So, if you have anything to say now is the time."
10:36 a.m.

"Randall, we are going to move the machine forward right now. It will move in the direction of the work bench."
11:14 a.m.

"Randall, I am going to present a thought to you. I've been told that you have strong religious and political convictions and principles that you have lived by. I understand that you would like others to adopt the same principles and convictions. Let's you and I be realistic about this situation.

On the one hand, if you make yourself available to arrest you can present your convictions in court. You will be big news for weeks, maybe months, worldwide, on television and in the newspapers.

On the other hand, if this situation ends violently and tragically, you and your convictions will be old news in two days. Instead of you and your convictions, the headlines will again be filled with all the evils of the world that your family and mine live in.

Let's you and I talk about it."
11:51 a.m.

"Randall, have you and Mrs. Weaver thought about arrangements for Samuel? I don't understand why you won't provide instructions to me. Help me to understand. Is it a violation of your convictions to talk to me and tell me what you want done for Samuel? Is that it? Samuel has been and will be treated with respect by the authorities but I don't know if we are doing the right thing. Help me. Help Samuel. Talk to me.

I'll wait 5 minutes for your response then we have to shut the machine down to cool off. After the machine has taken a break, I'll call you back."

> *Negotiator's comment: Randall Weaver appeared to be very into words. In a shed I found a book where he had written in big, bold, block letters, "righteousness = the right thing." So, I used the phrase "the right thing" several times. During a later conversation with Bo Gritz, Weaver said that he was not a "human" being because hue means color. Weaver said he is not a colored man. He is a white man.*

11:58 a.m.

Weaver was told that the robot was being shut down to cool off.

1:16 p.m.

> *Negotiator's comment: People had told us that Mrs. Weaver was the tough one and the strength of the family, so negotiators addressed many remarks to her having no inkling or clue whatever that she had been killed.*

"Mrs. Weaver, I'm sure you have concern for little Elizabeth. I share your concern. Is there anything I can get for her that would take that worry off your mind? Do you need milk, food, or diapers for her? Please talk it over with Randall and I'll do what I can for you. If there is anything I can do to ease your burden and concern for Elizabeth, let me know just by calling out."

1:59 p.m. (twice) and a third time at 2:21 p.m.

"Mrs. Weaver, you've had some time to talk to Randall about my offer to provide milk, food, and diapers for Elizabeth. As I have daughters of my own, I share your concern for the children. What do you want to do?"

4:27 p.m.

"Mr. Weaver, I wanted you to know that the APC is coming forward. The APC means you no harm but it is coming forward."

6:11 p.m.

"Mrs. Weaver, whatever yours and Randall's convictions with regard to the government, the courts, and the police, we have a common concern in the children. Let's not make their health and welfare an issue. Send them out and I will make sure that they sleep tonight in the home of your choosing. I'll ensure the well-being of your children as I'm sure you would look after mine. We both want to do the right thing by the children.

Talk to me about it."

8:09 p.m.

"Randall, let's talk about your convictions, your future, and the future of your family.

A history of this situation will be written in the next few days. The question is, who will make and write that history? Will it be you in a courtroom with sufficient time to fully express your views or will it be a secondhand story, written by someone else?

Randall, I don't know your intentions but I've been told that you are willing to die in defense of your convictions. I admire that strength. I'd like to think I would have that kind of courage. Randall, if you have told people you are willing to die, I believe you, but you don't have to die for your convictions. Live for your convictions. Live to tell your story to the world and to your grandchildren—the children of Sara, Rachel, and Elizabeth. Live to educate your children and your children's children. You and I know in our hearts it's the right thing to do.

What do you think? Talk to me."

9:47 p.m.

"Randall, I've told you before, I don't know what your intentions are in this situation but I think real courage is living to face adversity. I think real courage is living to maintain your convictions through all adversity. Set an example of courage to your children by coming out unarmed and facing your adversary in open court.

You may not believe the courts of the U.S. have authority over you but if you think about it no one who believes as you do has ever had the opportunity you now have. If you had $1 million you couldn't buy the publicity for your cause that you will receive by just having the courage to walk out of the house unarmed.

Please do it Randall."

Tuesday, 8/25/92

> *Negotiator's comment: When I arrived on scene there was only one other experienced negotiator present, Special Agent Wilson Lima, and his negotiation experience was limited. I wanted a negotiator at the forward Command Post 24 hours a day and Wilson graciously manned the midnight shift without a grumble. However, we virtually shut down the negotiations at night in an attempt to avoid possible sleep-deprivation problems.*
>
> *During the weekend, Special Agent Ed Burke arrived. My colleague and friend at the FBI Academy, now Unit Chief Gary W. Noesner urged that I bring in additional negotiators so I asked for Special Agents James Botting and John Dolan. All of the team's negotiators were talented agents and, more importantly, great people. Jim and John arrived on Tuesday.*

10:02 a.m. and 10:08 a.m.
"Randall, this is Fred. Good morning.

I thought you might like to know that we're taking care of your dog— the one with the mismatched eyes. The last time I saw him he was eating a big plate of spaghetti. We're calling him "JJ" because he looks like one of the guys that's with me.

> *Negotiator's comment: I tell my students to avoid using humor during a negotiation. I was not trying to be funny here but attempting to lighten the monologue. Weaver later told Bo Gritz that I was not taking the situation seriously apparently because of this statement. Nothing could have been further from the truth.*

Once again, let me know if Elizabeth needs anything.

Over the next few days I hope to demonstrate to you, Mrs. Weaver, and Kevin that despite all that's happened, everything is being done to ensure that this situation ends without further violence."

11:02 a.m.

"Randall, this is Fred.

I live in Virginia and until a couple of days ago I had not heard of your religious convictions and beliefs. Even today, all I know is the government's version of what they say are your religious beliefs.

I'd like to know what is going on here. I feel frustrated when you, Mrs. Weaver, and Kevin refuse to talk to me because I want to work this out with you.

Randall, these people are not going to go away. It may take a few days to prove that to you but if that's what it takes, they are prepared to do it.

Talk to me Randall, so you and I can start working on something and perhaps spare Rachel, Sara, and Elizabeth a few days of discomfort. Let's you and I begin resolving this situation peacefully. I'll talk to you later.

Randall, one last thing, I was just handed a tape-recorded message from Mrs. Weaver's family. I'll play that for you."

12:14 p.m.

"Mrs. Weaver, Randall, this is Fred.

I am going to play a tape-recorded message from some of your family members. I hope you can hear this message okay. I've only got a small recorder and it might be hard to understand. I'll play it now.

(Taped messages played.)

I hope you could hear that. I'll play it again when I get a better recorder in the hope that you will be able to hear it better.

I'll talk to you later. Remember, all you have to do is call out to our robot and I'll be able to hear you.

The APC ran over my original phone. I'm trying to get another phone for you."

1:03 p.m.

"Randall, let me tell you what is happening out here. First, I'm trying to get a better tape recorder. The guys out here told me they couldn't hear the message so you probably couldn't either.

Secondly, they are going to put a better speaker in place so that you'll be able to hear me more clearly. The speaker, when I get it, will be dropped off by the APC.

Lastly, I'm trying to get another telephone to put in front of your house.

That's what is going on out here. I hope all is well inside. Talk to you later."
1:37 p.m.
Weaver was told that an APC is coming up the hill. It meant him no harm. It will be in the front yard.
3:20 p.m.
"Randall, I'd like to hear from you about what happened the other day. Apparently, you have told people you would defend your property. Is that what you were doing— defending your property? What happened?

There's not only me that would like to know what happened. A whole lot of people would like to hear your side of the story. Tell your story Randall. Tell your story to the world. Tell it to me. Tell it to the media. Tell it in court. I know you've got a story to tell. Do it. You've got people's interest and curiosity. Now is the time to tell your story.

Before I leave, is there anything I can get for the kids—food, medicine, milk, diapers? If there is anything, just call out.

Talk to you later."
4:19 p.m.
"Mrs. Weaver, this is Fred.

I want to talk to you about your family. I assure you that no one out here means any harm to you or your family. Everyone is, of course, most concerned about Sara, Rachel, and Elizabeth. As a mother, I'm sure that one of your hopes for your daughters is that they grow up to raise children of their own. Help fulfill that dream by sending them out.

I'm telling you that when your daughters come out, whether it be tonight or five days from now, they will sleep in the home of people of your choosing.

As I told Randall, just speak out to the robot."
5:24 p.m.
"Mrs. Weaver, this is Fred.

Mrs. Weaver, I've been told by several people that you are the kind of wife who will stick with her husband through rough times. That's an admirable quality, but allow me to present you with a thought. We have no arrest warrant for you. You've done nothing illegal. Think about what you could do for your husband if you came out with your children tonight. You could tell your side of the story. You could tell what happened at the shooting. You could be talking to the media tonight. Couldn't you do more for your husband and for your convictions by going down the mountain with your children?

Please think about it Mrs. Weaver, and let me know what you want to do."

A short time later

"Mrs. Weaver, I'm about to play the tape again. I hope you can hear it better this time.

(Taped messages played again.)

I hope all is well inside. I'll talk to you later."

9:15 p.m.

"Mr. Weaver, this is Wilson (Lima).

Fred is gone for a little while. He asked me to give you a call. I am sure you had a lot to think about and also to talk about since Fred last talked to you. We are still very much interested to hear your side of the story. It is not too late. You can do it tonight. All it takes is for you, Mr. Weaver, and Kevin Harris to come out, unarmed. Do this for your convictions. Do this for your children. Do this for your wife. Do this for yourself, Mr. Weaver. You and Kevin Harris come out now, unarmed."

Wednesday, 8/26/92

4:33 a.m.

"Randall Weaver, this is Wilson. Good morning.

We are still waiting to hear from you. I've been thinking about you and your family all night long.

Is everyone well inside? Is there anything I can do for you? Please let me know.

This is a new day, Randall. Show your family that you care. You and Kevin come out, unarmed—come out and tell the world about your cause. This is the right time, Randall."

6:00 a.m.

"Vicki Weaver—This is Wilson. Good morning.

We all know that behind every successful man there is a strong woman. A woman of principles—a strong believer in your cause. You are the motivating force behind Randall. As an intelligent woman, I am sure you realize that the sooner Randall solves this problem, the better it will be for him, for the family, and for the cause. Please encourage Randall to come out, unarmed. Also encourage Kevin to do the same. They will listen to you. It will be a noble gesture on their part. People from all over will always remember this moment. There is a time and place for everything under the sun. This is the right time for Randall and Kevin to come out. Mrs. Weaver, please support them to come out now."

Later

"Vicki—You and I know that the race not always belongs to the swiftest—but to the smartest. Do the smart thing—encourage your husband, Randall, and Kevin to come out, unarmed. Encourage them to race and face the courts—to spread your convictions.

This situation will eventually be over—it is up to you to make the best out of it. By encouraging Randall and Kevin to come out, unarmed, you will be sharing with them the joy of spreading your beliefs. By coming out, unarmed, they will not be hurt.

I am concerned about you all. I want this situation to be solved peacefully—I'm sure you want the same. Are the children all right? Can we get some milk for Elizabeth? Let me know if I can be of any help by just calling out."

Mid-morning

"Randall, good morning. This is Fred.

Shortly, the APC will be approaching your home for the purpose of transferring the telephone to the robot. This may take some time. Again, you've got no cause for alarm. You've got my word on it."

12:27 p.m.

Weaver was told that the robot would be approaching the house with the telephone.

1:27 p.m.

Weaver was told that the robot has the telephone and we requested that he take the telephone from the robot.

2:05 p.m.

"Randall, I can understand your concern about the telephone and I can also understand why you might not want to step outside onto the front porch. So, here is what they are going to do. The robot will go to the window on the right side of the porch. The grippers will try [to] push the telephone through the window. The glass will break. After the telephone is delivered, the robot will back off the porch.

Randall, up until now you have not had a good way to talk to me. Let's take advantage of this opportunity to get a constructive dialogue going.

You've got nothing to worry about here."
2:08 p.m.
We made a correction to the previous statement. Weaver was told that the telephone would come through the door window not the window on the right side of the porch.
2:08 p.m.
Unidentified male voice later identified as that of Randall Weaver (RW): "Get the fuck out of here."
2:15 p.m.
Weaver was told that we now had a good opportunity for dialogue.
2:16 p.m.
Weaver makes unintelligible response. Weaver was told that he could not be heard.
2:17 p.m.
Weaver makes unintelligible response.
RW: "Get out of here."
RW: "... this kike son of a bitch."
RW: "Fucking pig."
Weaver was told he could not be heard.
2:19 p.m.
RW: "Get the fuck out of here."

> *Negotiator's comment: I had never been so delighted to get cussed out in all my life. To me, it had the sweet sound of progress though I am sure that is not what Weaver intended.*

2:20 p.m.
RW: "Lying motherfuckers."
2:21 p.m.
FL: I understand your anger. Let's try to resolve this.
2:23 p.m.
FL: Let's try to start anew.
2:27 p.m.
FL: Is Vicki close by? We will play a taped message to Vicki.
2:39 p.m.
FL: We are having a technical problem with the tape recorder.

2:45 p.m.
We played tape message from Vicki's family.
2:48 p.m.
FL: Your supporters and family are concerned about you and we want to start dialogue. Please pick up the telephone.
2:49 p.m.
Taped messages were played but perimeter personnel could not hear them.
2:50 p.m.
The taped message was replayed.
2:53 p.m.
FL: Please pick up the telephone.
2:55 p.m.
RW: "I ain't taking no goddamn telephone."
2:56 p.m.
Weaver is heard to say he wants to give sister and somebody else his story.
2:57 p.m.
FL: I heard "sister" and somebody else?
FL: We spoke to your father earlier.
2:57 p.m.
RW: Is father here?
2:58 p.m.
FL: I don't know if he is here now.
2:58 p.m.
FL: None of your relatives are here yet.
2:58 p.m.
RW: I want to speak to my sister.
3:00 p.m.
FL: We will try to locate your sister.
RW: Unintelligible
3:00 p.m.
FL: I can't hear you.
3:01 p.m.
RW: I want my sister to come here.
3:11 p.m.
FL: I just made a telephone call. Is your sister Marnis Joy?
3:12 p.m.
RW: She lives in Iowa.

3:14 p.m.

FL: Is there anyone local who knows Marnis Joy's telephone number?

> *Negotiator's comment: I advocate to my students that they avoid lying in a negotiation and this occasion was the only time I lied to Randall Weaver. We had located and interviewed Marnis Joy previously but if Randall Weaver was talking we wanted to keep him talking.*

3:22 p.m.
FL: I will be off air
3:24 p.m.
RW: Fine.
3:57 p.m.
FL: " Randall, this is Fred. I've got some people working on locating Marnis Joy in Iowa. I'll let you know as soon as I hear anything. Meanwhile, is there anything I can get for you, Mrs. Weaver, Kevin, or your girls?"
3:57 p.m.
RW: Unintelligible.
3:58 p.m.
FL: I can't hear you.
3:59 p.m.
RW: "... my sister..."
3:59 p.m.
RW: I want my sister.
4:00 p.m.
RW: No, no.
5:02 p.m.
FL: "Randall, can you hear me O.K.?

I told you earlier I would keep you informed. Well, we've located a friend of your sister in Jefferson, Iowa. He is out right now trying to find Marnis.

Please be thinking about how you want to get this phone in to talk to Marnis.

Let me know if you can hear me."
5:04 p.m.
RW: I can hear you. No phone.

5:05 p.m.
   RW: I want my sister here in person.
   FL: How can we do this?
   RW: Unintelligible
5:06 p.m.
   FL: How can we do this?
   FL: Couldn't we do this more safely for you and your sister?
   RW: Unintelligible
   RW: No phone.
5:07 p.m.
   RW: "I want my sister."
5:08 p.m.
   RW: "You guys are trigger happy."
5:09 p.m.
   FL: Think about how you and your sister can communicate safely.
5:11 p.m.
   FL: Just think about how to do it safely. Did you hear?
   RW: Yes, I heard you.
6:14 p.m.
   FL: "A concern out here is that if speak to your sister, you will tell your story to her, and then commit suicide. Randall, is that your intent? Are you going to commit suicide?

You are going to have to promise me that you will not harm your family or yourself. I've got to get an answer from you so I can relay it back."

> *Negotiator's comment: Any time a negotiator is concerned about suicide, he or she should ask about it directly. After the first day or so, my concern about suicide or homicide/suicide had receded but I had not totally ruled it out.*

6:17 p.m.
   RW: "I promise you no one will be hurt."
   RW: "I promise you no one will be hurt."
6:18 p.m.
   RW: I want my sister by the back door.

> *Negotiator's comment: It never ceases to amaze me how the little things can so thoroughly mess things up. In this*

case, I did not know which door he considered the "back" door. There were two doors to the house and one looked no more like the back door than the other. To make things worse, when Marnis arrived she did not know which door he considered the back door either. When she questioned Weaver about it, I got the impression he thought she was now on "our side."

6:20 p.m.
FL: I don't know if we can do that.
7:08 p.m.
FL: "Randall, I thought you might like to know that we have located Marnis. As you and I speak someone is talking to her about coming out here.
Can you hear me?"
7:09 p.m.
RW: "Yeah."

Negotiator's comment: I recommended to the on-scene commander that Randall Weaver's sister Marnis Joy be brought to the scene. I also recommended that an FBI Special Agent negotiator travel with her so he could make an assessment of her and her potential usefulness to the situation. I also wanted her to be assured that we were making a good-faith effort to end this incident without further violence.

She was flown to the scene aboard a chartered jet with her boyfriend, Mike Mumma who was the Weaver family attorney, and an FBI agent/negotiator. It was her first time aboard an airplane and it cost the taxpayers $10,000. I mention the cost only to point out the sense of urgency and extremes to which the FBI was going at this point.

8:20 p.m.
FL: "Randall, I have just learned that Marnis has agreed to talk to you and she will be traveling out here. Her travel arrangements are being made and she will be here tomorrow. In the meantime, if I get any additional information I'll let you know."
8:22 p.m.
I repeated 8:20 p.m. message.

Thursday, 8/27/92

9:56 a.m.

John Dolan (JD): Randall, this John. Can you hear me?

RW: Yes

JD: Your sister has arrived in Coeur D'Alene and she will be en route here. Understand me?

RW: Yes

9:57 a.m.

JD: Do your children need anything?

> *Negotiator's comment: Some tactical team members suggested that I call Randall, "Randy" as many townspeople did. I did not want to call him Randy because I wanted to stay more formal with him and I did not think he would like me getting too "chummy" with him. Secondly, I did not know how he felt about the name Randy. When Marnis arrived, she referred to Randall as "Pete." I asked why she called him Pete and she said that the townspeople call him Randy and he hates the name. The only person he allowed to call him Randy was Vicki. I never called him Randy.*

11:41 a.m.

FL: "This is Fred. I am taking you at your promise. Marnis ready to talk to you. Can you hear me?"

11:42 a.m.

FL: Get in a location where you can hear.

11:43 a.m.

RW: "... back door ..." Marnis, can you hear? They're playing games. Don't believe a goddamn thing they're saying.

11:49 a.m.

RW: Marnis ... last Saturday ... and they're afraid to let the truth out.

11:50 a.m.

Marnis Joy (MJ): I have Mike with me. ... help you and love you.

11:51 a.m.

RW: Unintelligible ... come in and kill someone.

11:53 a.m.

MJ: Brother, I'm going to tell you the truth. Mumma called me at home. I tried to do right. I brought Mike. Said would not be around. My brother...sending my love. I tell you. I have studied about Yahweh. Study books. Changed my life. Don't let me down. You know what's right. I brought Mike with me so we could do that.

Negotiator's notes: Our negotiator's notes are fragmentary because we were taking notes as fast as we could and she was speaking rapidly.

11:55 a.m.
Unintelligible. Same voice.
11:58 a.m.
MJ: Take phone. I'm hard of hearing from machines at work. I don't want to miss a word. Go get that phone. I can't hardly hear you. Pick up the phone. I want to hear what you have to say.

Negotiator's comment: Negotiators viewed Marnis Joy's hearing condition as a serious setback. She had visited Idaho the previous summer and not mentioned her hearing loss to Weaver. Now, she was saying the same thing we were saying, that is, that he could not be heard and please pick up the telephone. We were certain that he thought she had gone over to "our side."

12:01 p.m.
MJ: I want to know how my babies are.
Girl's voice: Unintelligible
12:02 p.m.
MJ: Sara. Rachel. Please get the phone. Marnis wants to talk to you. I want to communicate.
12:03 p.m.
Girl's voice: Unintelligible
12:04 p.m.
MJ: Take time. I want you on phone. I can hear girls talking. I want more.
12:15 p.m.
MJ: Brother, I've been trying to think how to get you to pick up the phone. Please, please, my family, tell me.
RW: No phone.
12:16 p.m.
MJ: Tell me if you're all okay.
RW: No, we're not.

Negotiator's comment: Though we wrote it down, none of us followed up on Randall's response until later in the day when I saw it in our negotiator's notes.

MJ: I need phone. It's just better for you and me, Honey.
12:17 p.m.
MJ: Brother, I've got your strong beliefs. I hope I stand tall as you do on your beliefs.
12:18 p.m.
MJ: I tried to. I hope I can help. What do you need? Tell me.
12:19 p.m.
MJ: Tell me what you need, Randall.
12:20 p.m.
MJ: I came to find out. I talked your religion. Tell me how I can help, help you.
12:22 p.m.
MJ: I want to tell you what happened since I got on the plane. He (an FBI agent) could talk the Bible. Study to go to ministry.
12:23 p.m.
MJ: Please pick up phone, please.
12:49 p.m.
MJ: Is robot in the front or back of the house?
12:50 p.m.
Marnis repeats the 12:49 question.
MJ: Is robot in front?
MJ: I need to get to where I can talk. Is robot in the front or rear?
12:52 p.m.
FL: We are confused, we want to make sure which side we are talking about.
12:53 p.m.
FL: Marnis told me that the last time she was here she didn't tell you about her hearing problem. We will work with you on this.
12:57 p.m.
FL: We want to get Marnis close to the house. We don't know what side you are talking about. Help us work this out. Please.
12:59 p.m.
FL: If I can work it out that Marnis approached the robot side of the house, is that agreeable?

1:00 p.m.
  RW: Unintelligible
1:01 p.m.
  FL: We can have Marnis approach the robot side of the house is that okay with you?
1:12 p.m.
  FL: Let me give you some options. We must establish better communications. You can have one of the girls take the phone into the house. It is a telephone. We wouldn't do anything in front of your sister. First option is have one of the girls pick up phone. Second option, Marnis and Fred get into APC and drive up to near vicinity of the robot. Talk it over.
1:14 p.m.
  FL: Let me know what you want to do.
1:27 p.m.
  FL: Marnis wants an answer. We brought her out here. She just told me she is not going down the hill without you and she'd talk it out. Talk to your sister.
1:37 p.m.
  FL: Please go to where you can hear me. You are having trouble trusting me. I can understand that but trust your own sister. Trust the sister you asked for. Give me an answer.
1:41 p.m.
  FL: Please go to where you can hear me. It seems this boils down to trust. You're going to have to trust somebody. You trusted her last night, trust her today. Take a risk on your sister.
1:43 p.m.
  FL: Talk to me about this.
1:44 p.m.

> *Negotiator's comment: I now tried another double bind. He would not talk to me but I did not think he would want us any closer to the house either. This time he responded.*

FL: Unless you tell me otherwise, Marnis and I will approach in the APC so we can get some communication going. This is our only reason for approaching the house and we will be approaching unless I hear from you otherwise. Talk to me.

1:46 p.m.

FL: We are taking your no response as your agreement to do this. Marnis and I will come forward in the APC in the next few minutes.

1:47 p.m.

RW: Back off Fred, back off.

FL: Good, we are not going to do anything to upset you or your family.

1:48 p.m.

FL: You've got your sister upset. She is sitting here in tears, tell me what I can tell her. Let's not spread this misery any further than it's already spread.

2:04 p.m.

FL: Marnis asked me to ask you if you had any Diet Pepsi in there. All we have out here is Diet Coke.

2:05 p.m.

FL: I guess you don't have any Diet Pepsi. How about if Marnis and I get into the APC, get behind the woodpile and the APC leaves?

RW: No.

2:06 p.m.

FL: Okay, I just heard you say no. Let's go to plan 137.

2:07 p.m.

FL: I've learned a few things about you. I know you have a military background. You are taking into consideration the tactical considerations. Tell us what you have in mind.

2:08 p.m.

RW: No. Unintelligible.

2:09 p.m.

FL: We got "no something." Tell us one more time.

FL: There is uncertainty. We will keep trying until you and I can sit down and work this out.

3:15 p.m.

FL: Just so you know, we are trying to get better equipment to hear you so we can talk. We'll give that a try.

3:16 p.m.

FL: Can you hear me?

3:17 p.m.

FL: Repeated above. Can you hear me?

3:19 p.m.

We repeated the 3:15 p.m. comment. We may try a new position. We'll get back to you in a few minutes.
3:38 p.m.

Marnis Joy, SA James M. Botting (JB) and I went to what the HRT had designated the "green" side of the house with a parabolic microphone. We could hear birds chirping but we were not sure if the "chirps" came from inside or outside of the house.

> *Negotiator's comment: Some tactical teams color code various sides of a building so there is no question as to what side of the structure they are referring to. We were negotiating from a position of cover and were on a virtual cliff. Marnis made several impassioned, tearful pleas that were met with silence. I deliberately "chewed out" Weaver for asking that his sister be brought to the scene and then breaking her heart by not talking to her. I told him I had heard he was a good family man, his sister was part of his family and he owed her an explanation and an apology. There was no response.*

4:58 p.m.

We all returned from the "green" side of the house after our failed attempts to open a dialogue with Weaver. All of our attempts were met with no response.

> *Negotiator's comment: Using a non-law enforcement person as an intermediary is always a potentially dangerous move but Marnis Joy could not have been better and that was bad news. I was thinking, "If she can't get to him, what will it take?"*

7:19 p.m.

FL: Randall, Vicki can you hear me? This morning when Marnis was talking and she asked if everyone was all right, you said "No." We have a doctor here if anyone needs a doctor. We are concerned about everyone, especially Elizabeth. Young kids can't take the punishment that adults can, if she needs anything, let us know.
7:21 p.m.

FL: Give me a sign you heard me.

FL: If you need anything just call out.
7:26 p.m.
I repeated the 7:19 p.m. statement.
11:25 p.m.
FL: Think about how we might better communicate tomorrow, as today was a disappointing day for both of us. Please give me some indication that you heard me.

Friday, 8/28/92

3:25 a.m.

Wilson Lima (WL): Randall, good morning, how are you? Is everyone all right? Thinking of you and your family, concerned about you and your family, very much concerned about Elizabeth. Is she okay? Does she need a doctor? We have a doctor out here. Does anyone need medical attention in there? Let me tell you this again, I care about them. I care about you. So let me know how I can help, speak out.

6:25 a.m.

WL: Randall, hello again. It's breakfast time. Do you have enough food there? You know it's going to be a hot day today, in the 80s. The kids probably would love to be outside. It's time for you all to come out. These people are going to be here until you all come out. They are not leaving. Make things easy for the kids. Let's solve this problem right now. People out here want to hear from you. We are all concerned about you, your wife, and the kids.

10:24 a.m.

Marnis Joy, Jim Botting, and I again went to the "green" side of the house in an effort to establish contact via bullhorn.

> *Negotiator's comment: The negotiation team was concerned that a repeat of the previous day's emotional experience would be too difficult for Marnis. We decided that if she could not accomplish anything before noon on this day, we would send her home. After she made an impassioned appeal to Weaver that resulted in no response, she said, "I am not doing you guys any good. I'll get out of your way and go home." (Not an exact quote.)*

10:36 a.m.

Marnis Joy spoke to Weaver via a bullhorn. Sorry I cried. I wish I knew what I could do. These guys are sincere and I have tried to make them understand. Let me know those kids are important to you. I am concerned about Kevin. I love you.

10:46 a.m.

Marnis talks about the children and asks Weaver to come out.

11:15 a.m.

Marnis again appeals to hear from someone. Wants peace and love and love in the house is strong. I love everyone. Tell me who you want to tell. You tell your story. This is traumatic to your family. Tell in your own words. I want to help you. I want to help anyway I can. Please talk to me so I know you are all right. Marnis has trouble hearing. Please talk to me. I'll talk to anyone.

12:23 p.m.

Radio personality Paul Harvey had commented on the incident in his broadcast and had urged Weaver to surrender. A tape recording of his broadcast was played.

12:25 p.m.

The Paul Harvey tape was repeated.

3:23 p.m.

JD: Notified Weaver that robot was moving rearward.

4:27 p.m.

JD: "Mr. and Mrs. Weaver, this is John. We didn't have to pull the robot back as we thought. This is not a trick. We want to bring the robot closer to the door to make it easier for you take the telephone. It is only a telephone. I understand that this may cause you some concern but it will make it safer and easier for you to take the telephone. We will do this shortly, please take the telephone."

RW: Back off, back off, we are not taking no goddamn telephone.

4:57 p.m.

JD: "Mr. and Mrs. Weaver, this is John again, we have moved the robot closer now. We are offering you another opportunity to accept the telephone. Please take the phone so that Vicki's father, Bo Gritz, John Reynolds, and others can talk to you. You can take it or one of the kids can take it. It is only a telephone."

4:59 p.m.

JD: Repeated 4:57 p.m. message.

5:15 p.m. (approximately)

RW: I will talk to Bo Gritz in person.
5:18 p.m.
JD: What do you mean in person?
5:25 p.m.
RW: I will talk to Bo Gritz in person, that's it or no more talking.
5:46 p.m.
JD: We are working on contacting Bo now. How are we to make communications any better?
5:48 p.m.
RW: He can come in through the back door.

> *Negotiator's comment: Bo Gritz had called in offering his services saying that Randall Weaver may have been in his U.S. Army unit at Fort Bragg and he may know him. Gritz was an unknown entity to me but Ed Burke knew the significance of Gritz to some right wingers. Based upon Burke's recommendation, I advocated to SAC Glenn that we use him.*
>
> *I went down the mountain in a four-wheel-drive vehicle to meet and pick up Gritz. Halfway back up the mountain I stopped the vehicle. Gritz and I got out for a talk. I told him that he was going to work with us and if he failed to cooperate and follow instructions, he would be going back down the mountain. He agreed to my conditions and we shook hands on it. To his credit, he cooperated fully.*

5:49 p.m.
JD: How are we going to improve communication?
JD: How are we going to improve communication?
5:57 p.m.
JD: Bo is not going to the back door because of safety. Let's devise a plan to talk safely. Let me know what you think.
6:01 p.m.
JD: Bo cannot go to the back door because of his safety. How will this be any different than with Marnis? Let me know.
6:04 p.m.
JD: Mr. and Mrs. Weaver we need to resolve this, we need to communicate better. Let me know.
6:06 p.m.

JD: Please talk to me, please talk to me, let me know.
6:08 p.m.
JD: What are you thinking about communicating?
6:15 p.m.
JD: Communications are terrible, we need to improve communication. Several people want to talk. We are going to place the telephone through the window.
6:17 p.m.
RW: Better not or it's all over asshole. Back off goddamn it, back off, son of a bitch. You've got my family upset, so back off.
A short time later
JD: Mr. and Mrs. Weaver, this is John. We will not move the robot any further, if you just establish a dialogue with us. Just talk with us about the situation, that is all we ask. Can we agree to this?
6:36 p.m.
JD: I've reached Bo Gritz, he will be coming up. Please give some thought to how you and your family with Bo's help can resolve this peacefully.
6:50 p.m.-6:55 p.m.

Bo Gritz attempted to talk to Weaver from the robot but once again it was very difficult, if not impossible, to hear Weaver. Bo Gritz spoke to Weaver on a variety of topics over the robot's bullhorn.

It was decided that Bo Gritz, HRT members and I would go forward, that is, closer to the house in the APC, so that we might be able to hear Weaver's responses.

A short time later

The APC approached the house and Gritz established his identity from the crew position at the top of the APC. I told Gritz to ask if everyone was all right inside the house. When he did, Randall said, "No."

I told Gritz, "Follow up on that." When he did, Randall said that Vicki was dead and that he and Kevin were wounded. I have never been so shocked in all my life. I had been "talking" to Vicki all week and I knew the obvious impact it must have had on the family.

As Gritz continued his attempts to establish a dialogue, we still could not hear Weaver's replies very well. Gritz, ASAC Rogers, and I then got out of the APC and Gritz attempted to speak to Weaver from a position of cover beside the APC. Hearing Weaver was still bordering on the impossible. Gritz then left his position of cover, went forward, and opened a dialogue with Weaver.

As FBI negotiators could not hear Weaver's side of these communications, they were not recorded in any way.

Saturday, 8/29/92

8:43 a.m.
JD: Randy, this John, Bo is coming up.
8:45 a.m.
RW: No bull horn. Speak man to man. Only way.
8:46 a.m.
JD: Understand, no bullhorn through window.

> *Negotiator's comment: When Bo Gritz arrived in the morning, Jackie Brown, who was a neighbor and friend of Vicki Weaver, accompanied him. A minister who described himself as a personal friend of Randall Weaver also accompanied Gritz. (I was later told that the minister lied to us in saying that Randall Weaver did not know him.) These individuals left their positions of cover and went forward with Gritz to speak via direct voice to Weaver. In the afternoon and into the night, Gritz and retired Phoenix police officer Jack McLamb spoke to Weaver from outside the house.*

Sunday, 8/30/92

Gritz and McLamb resumed discussions with Weaver and at approximately 1:30 p.m., Kevin Harris surrendered. He was checked by paramedics and flown to the hospital via helicopter. Jack McLamb accompanied Harris to the hospital.

Gritz returned to the house. On this occasion, he agreed to wearing a body transmitter and he was again accompanied by Jackie Brown. This was the first time I heard Randall Weaver talk in conversational tones. To me, he sounded frighteningly unstable. For example, it was at this point that Weaver made his "I'm-not-a-human-being" point.

Later that same day, Gritz and Brown removed Vicki Weaver's body from the residence in a body bag. Upon his return, McLamb went into the Weaver residence with Gritz.

The negotiation team strongly suspected that there would be an assault that night but no one told us why it was being considered. To this day, I do not know why the HRT came so close to an assault.

At one point, I stopped SAC Robin Montgomery by putting my hands on both his shoulders. I told him that if he was going to authorize an entry that he might have to testify in court some day as to why an entry was not appropriate a week ago but it was appropriate now. In other words, he must be able to verbalize with specificity what had changed in the incident to make tactical action necessary. I believe this concept is absolutely crucial in crisis management's "go, no go" decision making.

Though I was concerned about the possibility of an assault, I did not want to display my apprehension to Bo. When the negotiation team approached him about planning the next day's negotiations, Gritz said, "Negotiations are out. Tactics are in."

That night, being relatively certain that we would no longer be needed, the negotiation team went into Sandpoint, ID to spend the night in a motel. I took my first hot shower in over a week and slept in a real bed. The following morning, I turned on the Cable News Network (CNN) to see what had happened at Ruby Ridge overnight. I was sure that if the HRT had made entry it would be on the news. Apparently, the siege was not over. We returned to Ruby Ridge and resumed our negotiation effort.

On our way back to Ruby Ridge, we passed a skinhead wearing a Nazi armband and attempting to hitch a ride. We jokingly considered giving this "Nazi" insult to my father's generation a ride to the roadblock with five FBI agents.

Monday, 8/31/92

9:35 a.m.

Bo Gritz and Jack McLamb went to the "black" side of the house. Both men were wearing body transmitters. An emergency assault word of "Alaska" was established and they would also indicate when the baby was in a safe location should a rescue be necessary. Before Bo Gritz and Jack McLamb went forward, negotiation options, surrender plans, and what to expect in the event of an emergency assault were discussed in detail.

10:00 a.m.

At this time, Gritz and McLamb were on the porch talking into the house. Weaver was told what Gritz had told media representatives. Specifically, Gritz told Weaver that Kevin was charged with murder and this news agitated Weaver significantly. It did not appear that Weaver was going to allow Gritz into the house. Gritz and McLamb remained on the porch.

> *Negotiator's comment: The negotiation team was concerned about the possibility that Gritz might take action on his own and attempt to physically subdue Weaver. We wondered if Weaver was concerned about the same possibility.*

10:26 a.m.

It has been agreed that the robot will withdraw. Gritz helped in the withdrawal of the robot and was asked to look at the shotgun so that he could later attest to the fact that it was unloaded. McLamb stayed with the Weavers.

> *Negotiator's comment: When the robot initially went forward, our only thought was to use it to safely move the telephone closer to the house. However, when it got close to the house we immediately saw the advantage of leaving it in place so we could take advantage of the closed-circuit television capability. We could also speak to Weaver over the loud hailer and, sometimes, we could hear Weaver when he called out. Additionally, as I had told Weaver, the terrain was very rough, even for a tracked vehicle, and we were afraid it would topple over if we attempted to move it away from the house.*

10:30 a.m.

The robot began its withdrawal and Gritz gave steering directions to the HRT operators of the robot.

11:00 a.m.

The robot withdrawal was completed.

11:05 a.m.

Gritz returned to the house. Meanwhile, Weaver had been trying to talk Sara into surrendering.

It was during this time period that Jack McLamb said what I believe to be the single most important sentence of the negotiation effort, "Bo and I are your guardian angels and we are here to protect you, but we've got to leave."

11:30 a.m.

Gritz and McLamb continued a dialogue with the Weavers in their house.

11:50 a.m.

Weaver and his daughters have been in a private conference for about five minutes.

11:53 a.m.

Weaver told Gritz and McLamb to tell the people down at the roadblock to go about their business and that they would be down in nine days.

12:16 p.m.

McLamb came back to the forward command post for five minutes to get a promise from SAC Gene Glenn and then returned to the residence. The promise was that McLamb and Gritz would be able to act as a shield and accompany the Weavers to a place of safety. The girls were promised that they would be allowed to return to their home by September 9, a day that is meaningful in their religious beliefs.

12:34 p.m.

The door on the "black" side of the house was opened and Gritz and McLamb entered the house.

As the end of the siege neared, I turned to one of the other negotiators and said, "Bet you $5 that when Weaver comes out he will be carrying the baby." I was sure that Weaver would still believe himself to be in danger and would be holding the baby for protection.

1:11 p.m.

When he came out of the cabin and descended the nearby hill he walked within a few feet of me. I realized that even though we had been in this struggle for more than a week, he would not recognize me. I was also thinking, "My God, he looks like a Nazi death camp survivor."

I noticed that he was carrying the baby.

The Aftermath

I have been asked if I considered the end result to be a negotiation victory. My partner, Gary Noesner, reminded me that not a shot was fired after we began the negotiation effort. I do not have to personally talk someone out to consider the resolution to be a negotiation success. However, with the deaths of Bill Degan, and Vicki and Samuel Weaver, the outcome was nothing any of us could celebrate.

A major disappointment came with the realization that we had let Bill Degan down. He was no part of some "New World Order" movement. He was no part of some governmental conspiracy. He was a family man doing his job just as I was doing mine.

On the first day back at my office, I received a telephone call. It was an FBI agent/negotiator who was helping a police agency with a hostage situation in a motel. He asked for my assistance with the incident and for the first time I realized how emotionally drained I was. It was a good thing that he did not need much because I had virtually nothing left to give. I was on empty and exhausted.

Some time after the siege, I received a telephone call from Mike Mumma, the Weaver family attorney in Iowa. Upon hearing his name, my first thought was that I was about to be sued. Instead, he said he was in his office with the Weaver family. (I do not know which members of the Weaver family.) He said that though others were getting all the publicity in the media, the Weaver family knew who the real hero of Ruby Ridge was and they wanted to thank me. I was so stunned, shocked, and overjoyed, I nearly fell out of my chair.

Bo Gritz sent me an autographed copy of his autobiography. On the inside cover, he wrote that Randall Weaver did not think much of me but that he, Bo, thought I was a hell of a guy.

Though there were certainly major crisis management problems at Ruby Ridge, nothing changed in the FBI's crisis management response. Nothing changed, that is, until another incident occurred in a small Texas city called Waco. In its aftermath, everything about the way the FBI conducts sieges changed and changed for the better.

Figure H.1 View from Randall Weaver's cabin.

Figure H.2 The hostage rescue team's robot was used in the attempts to open a dialogue with Randall Weaver, maintain a video surveillance of the residence and as a delivery vehicle for the telephone.

A Negotiator's View of the Incident at Ruby Ridge 201

Figure H.3 The FBI's negotiation team. From left to right are John Dolan, James Botting, Frederick J. Lanceley and Ed Burke. (Not pictured is Wilson Lima.)

Figure H.4 The FBI used Bo Gritz as an intermediary.

Figure H.5 The Weaver cabin sat at the top of Ruby Ridge.

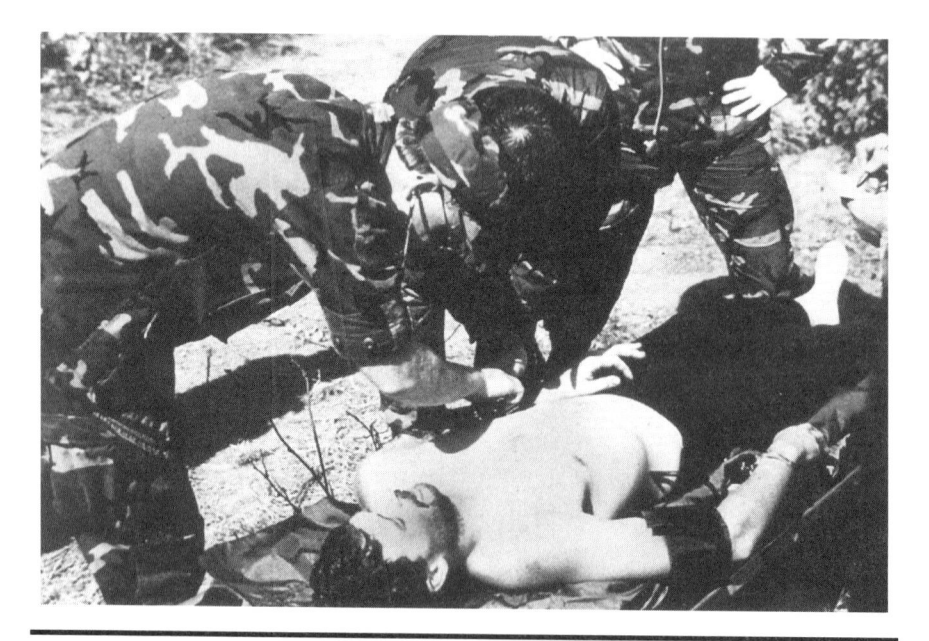

Figure H.6 Kevin Harris was provided on-scene medical assistance upon his surrender.

Figure H.7 Sarah Weaver, with clenched fist, exited the residence.

Figure H.8 Bo Gritz accompanies Randall Weaver and Elisheba from the Weaver cabin.

Index

A

Abandonment, 101
Abnormal psychology, for crisis negotiators, 95-115
   antisocial personality disorder, 96-99
      characteristics, 97-98
      common behaviors, 98
      communication suggestions, 98-99
   borderline personality disorder, 99-103
      characteristics, 100
      course, 101
      familial pattern, 101
      common behaviors, 101-102
      communication suggestions, 102-103
   major depressive episode, 111-115
      associated features, 111
      common behaviors, 112-114
      communication suggestions, 114-115
      course, 112
      culture and gender features, 111-112
      treatment, 114
   schizophrenia, 103-111
      age of onset, 106
      associated features, 106
      common behaviors, 109-110
      communication suggestions, 110-111
      complications, 106-107
      course, 108
      definitions, 104-105
      familial pattern, 108
      impairment, 106
      personality prior to illness, 107
      predisposing factors, 107
      prevalence, 108
      sex ratio, 108
      treatment/medication, 109
Achille Lauro hijacking, 138
Active listening, 17-24
   assumptions, 17-18
   concepts, 18-20
   emotion labeling, 20-21
   I messages, 23
   minimal encouragers, 22
   open-ended question, 23-24
   paraphrasing, 21-22
   reflecting or mirroring, 22
   silence, 22
   skills, 20, 53
Active listening techniques, overview of, 133-134
   emotion labeling, 133
   I message, 134
   minimal encouragers, 134
   open-ended questions, 134
   paraphrasing, 133
   reflecting or mirroring, 133
   silence, 134

Adrenaline, 69
Aircraft hijacking, 23, 89
Alcohol
    effect of over time, 56
    providing, 46
Ammunition, used in sieges, 8, 11
Anger, 36, 106, 180
Antipsychotic medications, 109
Antisocial personality disorder, 95, 96, 97
Anxiety, 106
    levels, dangers of manipulating, 141-143
    manipulating, 73
    techniques, 141
APC, see Armored personnel carrier
Armored personnel carrier (APC), 163, 177, 189
Aryan Nation, 160
ASAC, see Assistant Special Agent in Charge
Assistant Special Agent in Charge (ASAC), 162, 194
Assistant United States Attorney (AUSA), 166
ATF, see Bureau of Alcohol, Tobacco, and Firearms
Auditory hallucinations, 110
AUSA, see Assistant United States Attorney
Autopsy, 170

B

Background noises, 62
Bank robber, 45, 46
Barricade(s)
    situation, 34, 107
    suicides as opposed to, 2
Barroom brawls, 14-15
Battle scars, 100
Behaviors, self-destructive, 15
Beliefs, strong, 187
Benzodiazepine tranquilizers, 28
Body armor, 44, 72
Booby trap, 165
Borderline personality disorder, 95, 99
Boredom, 55

Brooding, 111
Bullhorn, 51, 86, 192
Burden, final, 13
Bureau of Alcohol, Tobacco and Firearms (ATF), 160

C

Cable News Network (CNN), 196
Cancer, terminal, 14
Carbon monoxide poisoning, 32
Career criminals, 49
Caring, demonstration of, 50
Chaplain, departmental, 18
Chemical agents, 44
Chest pains, 69
Chicken scratches, 29
Childhood backgrounds, 98
Clergy, 78
Closed-ended questions, 24
CNN, see Cable News Network
Command Post (CP), 162, 163, 168
Communication
    common means of, 51
    recommendations, 62
Containment, 44
Contingency plans, 56
Convictions
    defense of, 174
    religious, 172
Corrections officers, 99
County Coroner, 170
CP, see Command Post
Crisis
    commercially built, 52
    intervention, see Crisis intervention, crisis states, and management
    enthusiasts, 155
    rule of thumb in, 47
    team, 45
    troubled state of, 153-155
    negotiation
        number one priority in, 43
        team, 82
    negotiators, see Abnormal psychology, for crisis negotiators

states, see Crisis intervention, crisis states and
Crisis intervention, crisis states and, 13-16
   crisis characteristics, 14-15
   crisis intervention, 15-16
   crisis state, 13-14
   purpose of crisis intervention, 16
Custodial disputes, 5

D

DARE, see Drug Abuse Resistance and Education
Deadlines, guidelines concerning, 57
Debriefing
   of responding officers, 84
   session, mandatory, 18
Delusions, 105, 108
Demands
   negotiators dealing with, 57
   presentation of, 58
Depression, 18, 106, 113
Dialogue, opportunity for, 180
Digestive system, disorders of, 69
Dispatcher, 55
Disturbance call, 33
Divorce, 26
Domestic disputes, 5
Domestic incidents, 7, 77
Domestic situation, 91
Double whammy, 38
Dragnet, 19
Drink, drugging, 46
Drug(s)
   effect of over time, 56
   trade involvement, 5
   use, 14
Drug Abuse Resistance and Education (DARE), 168

E

Early morning awakening, 30
Eating binges, 15
Eccentric dress, 106

Embassy takeover, by terrorists, 3
Emergency
   assault
      what to expect in event of, 197
      word, 196
   personnel, 137
Emotion(s)
   labeling, 20, 21, 133
   presence of, 21
Emotional problems, 18
Emptiness, chronic feelings of, 102
Encouragers, minimal, 22
Entry teams, live coverage of, 75
Ethical considerations, 78
Exhaustion
   leading to fuzzy thinking, 54
   of negotiators, 93

F

FAA, see Federal Aviation Administration
Face-to-face negotiations, 72
Facts, emotional message behind, 19
Family values, 80
Fantasy, disruption of by negotiator, 41
Fate, role of, 32
FBI, 142
   Academy, 175
   agent, 96, 187
   instructors, 1
   negotiator, 3, 103, 169
   Special Agent in Charge (SAC), 154, 163
   Special Agent negotiator, 184
Federal agents, armed, 167
Federal Aviation Administration (FAA), 76
Federal government, paranoid grievance against, 137
Financial difficulties, 13
Firearm(s)
   intended suicide by, 40
   training records, 155
Food, drugging, 46
Forward Command Post, 168
Four-wheel-drive vehicle, 193

G

Gambling, 102
Go, no go decision making, 196
Gunman, teenage, 2
Gustatory hallucinations, 105

H

Hallucinations, 104, 105, 110
Hanging, suicide by, 40
Heart attacks, 69
Helicopter, 163
Helplessness
  expressions of, 26
  feelings of, 28
Hesitation marks, 29
Hijacking(s)
  Achille Lauro, 138
  aircraft, 23, 89
  completed, 65
  incompleted, 65
Homelessness, 98
Homicide/suicide, 142, 183
Hopelessness, 112
  expressions of, 26
  feelings of, 28
Hospital, forensic, 107
Hostage(s)
  abuse of by subject, 67
  ambivalent feelings of, 68
  contact between subject and, 66
  definition of, 3
  injuries, 65
  negotiators, 2, 25
  Rescue Team (HRT), 161
  takers, 8, 59
  value, 4
Hostage negotiation, 43-94
  before deviating from guidelines, 90
  boss as negotiator, 81-82
  common means of communication, 51-53
  common subject weaknesses, 68-69
  communication recommendations, 62
  concerns arising with passage of time, 54-5
  containment, 44
  courses of action, 43-44
  crisis negotiation team, 82-85
  deadlines, 57
  demands, 57-59
  double checking of intelligence, 62-63
  effects of negotiating on negotiators, 91-94
    possible long-term stressors/problems, 93-94
    possible short-term stressors and problems, 91-93
  exposed face-to-face considerations, 71-73
  hostage injuries, 65
  indicators of negotiation progress, 74
  manipulation of anxiety, 73
  medical problems in high-stress situations, 68
  negotiating non-negotiable situation, 88
  negotiator's relationship to hostages and victims, 67-68
  non-response situations, 63-65
  perimeters, 44-45
  potential problem areas with media, 75-76
  potential problem words and phrases, 73
  priorities, 43
  role of time, 53
  situation boards, 87-88
  stalling techniques, 53-54
  Stockholm Syndrome, 65-67
  subject's needs, 59-62
  suggested negotiator introduction, 48-51
  supplies and equipment for ready kit, 85-86
  surrender, 88-90
  tactical role of negotiator, 86-87
  taping of negotiation, 70-71

Index

telephone negotiation techniques, 70
use of third-party intermediaries, 77–81
what is negotiable, 45–48
HRT, see Hostage Rescue Team
Human life, preservation of, 43
Husband
   abusive, 64
   estranged, 63
Hyperventilation, 69

I

Identity disturbances, 101
I messages, 32, 134
Incident
   domestic, 77
   early hours of, 49
   hostage-taking, 74
   medical problems during, 55
   at Ruby Ridge, 142, 159–203
Injuries, self-inflicted, 100
Innocents, involvement of in siege, 8
Insomnia, extreme, 30
Intelligence support person, 84
Interview guide, for investigators, 125–129
   coping with stress, 128
   current stressors, 128
   descriptive information, 126
   drug/alcohol history, 126–127
   educational level, 126
   friends, relatives, and others close to person, 129
   indicators of impulsivity, 126
   interests, 128
   mental-health history, 127
   occupational history, 128
   relationship to victim, 128
   similar incidents, 126
   subject background, 125
   suicide, 127
   weapons information, 126
Irritability, 111

J

Jumper, 40

K

Kidnapping
   known location, 5, 6
   statute, federal, 3
   types of, 3
   unknown location, 4, 6

L

Labeling, emotion, 20, 21
Language differences, 64
Law enforcement
   agencies, 55
   executives, 82
   loss of control of, 79
   negotiators, 2, 42
   officers
      FBI's annual report on, 154
      killed, 35
   personnel, 25, 26
Lifestyle, stressful, 93
Listening
   active, see Active listening
   skills, 20
LSD, 41

M

Major depressive episodes (MDE), 111
MDE, see Major depressive episodes
Media
   attention, 56, 110
   personnel, 76
   potential problem areas with, 75
Medical assistance, on-scene, 202
Medical problems, in high-stress situations, 68
Mental health professional (MHP), 15, 85, 95
   assistance of, 96

elderly, 48
ethics of, 78
patients interviewed by, 99
Messages, taped, 178, 181
MHP, see Mental health professional
Microphone, parabolic, 190
Military services, 98
Miranda warnings, 71
Mirroring, 22, 133
Morale, 51
Motivation
    determination of for committing suicide, 36
    for spontaneous sieges, 10
Mutual-aid pacts, 153

N

Name, use of disrespectful form of, 50
Negative contact, 67
Negotiation(s)
    avoiding lying in, 182
    effort, 147-149
    face-to-face, 72
    fanatics, 93
    progress, indicators of, 74
    responsibilities, 149
    taping, 70
    techniques, telephone, 70
Negotiator(s)
    boss as, 81
    common psychological problem of, 92
    crisis, see Crisis negotiators
    dealing with demands, 57
    disruption of fantasy by, 41
    distrust of, 148
    effects of negotiating on, 91
    exhaustion of, 93
    FBI, 3, 103
    feelings of responsibility of, 94
    frustrated, 92
    hostage, 2, 25
    introduction, suggested, 48
    law enforcement, 2, 42
    low-ranking, 81
    notes, 186

primary, 83
qualities, 42
relationship of to hostages and victims, 68
secondary, 83
tactical role of, 86
technique to pressure subjects into talking to, 141
Neighbor, killing of, 13
New World Order movement, 199
New York City Police Department (NYCPD), 1
Nodding out, 46
Non-response situations, 63
NYCPD, see New York City Police Department

O

Oklahoma City, bombing in, 137
Olfactory hallucinations, 105
On-scene commanders, 83
Open-ended questions, 23, 134

P

Parabolic microphone, 190
Paramedics, 195
Paranoia, 59, 142
Paraphrasing, 21, 133
People skills, 17
Perimeters, 44
Personality disorders, commonly diagnosed, 95
Perspective, problem in, 1-6
    crisis negotiators responding to variety of situations, 1-3
    definitions, 3-4
    kidnapping, 3
        known location, 5-6
        unknown location, 4-5
Police
    departments, 1
    procedures, 79
Political convictions, 172
Positive contact, 66
Prisoner, 61

Index

Profanity, 62
Promiscuous sex, 15
Psychological pain, build-up of, 14
Psychomotor retardation, 114
Public attention, 56
Purposeful timing, 8

Q

Questions
    closed-ended, 24
    open-ended, 23, 134

R

Radio broadcast, 147
Rapport-building, 51
    atmosphere, 49
    efforts, 143
Ready kit, supplies for, 85
Reckless driving, 14
Reflecting, 22, 133
Religious considerations, 5
Religious convictions, 172
Robot
    bullhorn, 194
    being shut down, 173
    speaking to, 177
    transferring telephone to, 179
    withdrawal of, 197
ROE, see Rules of Engagement
Romance, broken, 34
Ruby Ridge
    incident at, 142
    negotiator's view of incident at, 159–203
Rules of Engagement (ROE), 162

S

S.W.A.T. team, 49, 90
SAC, see FBI Special Agent in Charge
Sadness, 18
Sarcasm, extreme, 102
Schizophrenia, 103
    forms of, 104
    prevalence of, 108
    sex ratio, 108
Self-image, unstable, 101
Self-loathing, 102
Self-mutilating behavior, 101
Serial killer, 97
Sexual abuse, 100
Sexual assault, 5
Sexual identity, 101
Sexual partners, history of, 97
Shift-change schedule, 75
Siege(s)
    location, 43
    deliberate, 8
    spontaneous, 9, 10
    types of, 7
Sieges, profiling, 7–11
    ammunition, 11
    approach, 9
    drugs/alcohol, 11
    duration, 9
    involvement of innocents, 8–9
    location, 10
    motivation, 10
    number of subjects, 10
    occurrence, 9
    preparation, 11
    purposeful timing, 11
    stance, 10
    state of mind, 10
    substantive demands, 8
    weapons, 11
Situation boards, 87
Sleep
    abnormalities, 111
    -deprivation problems, 175
Snipers, 76, 164
Social isolation, 109
Stalling techniques, 53
State of mind, in sieges, 8, 10
Stockholm Syndrome, 65, 66
Stress
    build-up, 14
    relieving, 15
Stressors, possible short-term, 91
Subject
    barricaded, 61
    borderline psychotic, 78

    contact between hostages and, 66
    in crisis state, 9
    exhaustion of, 54
    expressive needs of, 60
    frightening, 143
    giving in to, 58
    needs of, 59
    reassurance from 31
    way to put pressure on, 148
    weaknesses, 68
Substantive demand, 4, 8
Suicide(s)
    attempts, history of, 102
    audience for vindictive, 48
    barricades as opposed to, 2
    clues, 26
    completion rate, 100
    -by-cop, 2, 38, 142
    family history of, 28
    intent
        communicating, 33
        determining, 27
        as problem-solving option, 33
        reasons people commit, 35
        romantic view of, 40
        situations, indicators of progress in, 39
        threat, 30, 35, 78
Suicide intervention, 25-42
    ambivalence, 36
    anger, 36
    basic concepts for crisis negotiators, 34-35
    calling time out in suicide situations, 39
    crisis intervention techniques, 40-42
    determining motivation, 36
    determining suicidal intent, 27
    exposed face-to-face in suicide situations, 39-40
    flow chart, 119-122
    hostage negotiators, 25-26
    indicators of progress in suicide situations, 39
    negotiator qualities, 42
    potential high-risk indicators, 28-31
        detailed suicidal threat, fantasy, or plan, 30

    experienced team's gut feeling, 30
    extreme insomnia, 20
    family history of suicide, 28-29
    finding person in isolated location, 29
    history of impulsivity, 28
    hopelessness and helplessness, 28
    increasingly dangerous suicidal gestures, 30
    presence of drugs and/or alcohol, 29
    psychological history, 30-31
    reassurance from subject, 31
    test-firing of weapon, 29
    reasons people commit suicide, 35-36
    strange stories and role of fate, 32-33
    suicide clues, 26-27
    suicide-by-cop, 37-39
    suicide as problem-solving option, 33
Surrender, 198
    ritual, 89
    subject wanting to, 88
Surveillance
    photographic, 86, 165
    video, 200
Sympathy, 18

T

Tactical back-up, 73
Tactical personnel, 153
Tactical teams, 147, 185
Tactile hallucinations, 105
Tape-recording capability, of telephones, 52
Tearfulness, 111
Teenage gunman, 2
Telephone(s)
    company security representative, 76
    cordless, 52
    negotiation techniques, 70

Index

systems, tape-recording capability of, 52
Television broadcast, 147
Terminal insomnia, 30
Terrorists, embassy takeover by, 3
Theology, as emotional minefield, 115
Therapists, opposite-sex, 107
Third-party intermediaries (TPI), 77
Threshold diagnosis, 169
Time, importance of passage of, 53
TPI, see Third-party intermediaries
Training, continuing need for, 137–138
Tranquilizers, benzodiazepine, 28
Truck driver, 14
Trust, 188

U

United States Marshal Service (USMS), 161
USMS, see United States Marshal Service

V

Values, 19, 80
Vehicle, remote-controlled, 169
Venting, 155
Verbal outbursts, 102
Verbal will, 37
Victims, relationships of negotiator to hostages and, 68
Video
  camera, 86
  surveillance, 200
Visual hallucinations, 104

W

Waco, 199
Weapon(s)
  accidental discharge of, 37
  test-firing of, 29, 47
  used in sieges, 8, 11
Whole body illness, 112
Witnesses, 84